PROFILES
★ ★ ★ IN ★ ★ ★
CHARACTER

PROFILES

✶ ✶ ✶ IN ✶ ✶ ✶

CHARACTER

THE VALUES THAT MADE AMERICA

BY MEMBERS OF THE
1994 CLASS OF THE
UNITED STATES CONGRESS

OLIVER
NELSON

THOMAS NELSON PUBLISHERS
Nashville • Atlanta • London • Vancouver

Published in Nashville, Tennessee, by Thomas Nelson, Inc., Publishers, and distributed in Canada by Word Communications, Ltd., Richmond, British Columbia.

Unless otherwise noted, the Bible version used in this publication is THE NEW KING JAMES VERSION. Copyright © 1979, 1980, 1982 Thomas Nelson, Inc., Publishers. Scripture quotations marked NASB are taken from THE NEW AMERICAN STANDARD BIBLE. Copyright © 1960, 1962, 1963, 1968, 1971, 1972, 1973, 1975, 1977 by The Lockman Foundation and are used by permission.

Unless otherwise noted, photographs in this book are the property of the persons depicted and are used by permission.

ISBN 0-7852-7356-5

Printed in the United States of America.

1 2 3 4 5 6 — 01 00 99 98 97 96

Contents

☆

FOREWORD

☆

William J. Bennett

Whatever is true," St. Paul wrote in his eloquent injunction to the Philippians, "whatever is honorable, whatever is right, whatever is pure, whatever is lovely, whatever is of good repute, if there is any excellence and if anything worthy of praise, let your mind dwell on these things" (4:8 NASB).

Profiles in Character gives us a lot to dwell on. It recounts the true and praiseworthy stories of impressive people—individuals such as William Wilberforce, William Booth, Elizabeth Newton, and Abraham Lincoln—as well as people who are less well-known, but admirable. In many of the lives profiled here, it is fair to say that there is a certain nobility, a dedication to a worthy end, that is embodied in their character and in their conduct. At its heart, this is a book that celebrates what is good and honorable in human affairs.

Profiles in Character is an unusual book, in both its content and its authorship. Each profile was written by a freshman member of the U.S. House of Representatives, in recognition of the power of moral example on his or her own life. This book is not intended to be political or partisan, but instructive—to showcase the triumph of personal goodness and celebrate the power of personal example. In acknowledging the importance of good character, it recognizes the limits of politics, and the need for good examples as well as good laws.

This books comes at an appropriate time. We live in a too

cynical age, a time characterized by trash television, academic relativism, tabloid journalism, and a near collapse of trust in our political institutions. During the last thirty years or so, in some quarters at least, it became *de rigueur* to scoff at virtue and question honor, and almost every modern-day role model and hero became an instant target for "demythologizing." For some people, the worst in human nature has become more real than the best—and it certainly seems to get more airtime. The degraded belief that every good action has an ulterior and crass motive has made real-life heroes invisible to us. And our lives, our civilization, are the uglier for it.

This is not to argue for naïveté; on the contrary, excellence of character is often seen most clearly in contrast to its opposite—behavior that is degraded, brutish, deceitful. Heroes are foils to the darker side of human nature. We cannot blind ourselves to either reality, but we cannot understand one without recognizing the other.

Attention to good character, to standards of right and wrong, even to the study of heroes, seems to be making a comeback. This is encouraging because heroes elevate not only the individual by dint of inspiration, but the larger society as well by reinforcing the ideas and virtues necessary for its continuance. In the *Politics*, Aristotle defined education as that which equipped students to discern the good from its counterfeit, and to prefer the former to the latter. Children need to know what deserves to be emulated and loved and nurtured, but knowledge of these things is not transmitted by genes; it must be taught. And perhaps the best way to teach it is to offer real-life examples of men and women who have demonstrated the kind of character we think they should possess.

There is a larger point to be made here, too: the study of heroes not only illuminates the reality of human potential; it also lifts up the human personality. It exalts that which is best in the human spirit, and encourages its replication. It demonstrates the dictum of Immanuel Kant, that you can prove the possible by the actual. The real-life people profiled here are actual; many of them are a walking illustration of the power of character and an encouragement to emulation.

Profiles in Character is a good book because it affirms good things. It showcases the triumph of good character in the lives of men and women, both famous and obscure. It reminds us of what is most important—that excellence of character trumps position, income, and education any day. Ultimately, it is a call for character in our own lives. The American people should read it, reflect on it, enjoy it, and learn from it.

INTRODUCTION

☆

Congressman Dick Armey

Character. This sometimes forgotten virtue is very much in the public mind as well as in the minds of our nation's political leaders, writers, and philosophers.

The titles populating our bookstores and best-seller lists reflect the deep public concern over the moral state of the country: *The Book of Virtues* (and its sequel, *The Moral Compass*), *Values Matter Most*, *The Things That Matter Most*, *The Moral Sense*, and so on.

To remind us of the importance of character, actor Tom Selleck and a host of other luminaries have gone so far as to form a group called Character Counts. Many of us are shocked that our civic life has deteriorated to the point that we require an organization so titled. But the truth is we do require it.

Despite America's unparalleled material prosperity, we all sense there is something not quite right in our country. That something is the deterioration of individual character, which, unchecked, leads to the national character crisis that fuels everything from rising crime rates to trash-talking in sports to political corruption.

The great Irish conservative Edmund Burke said two centuries ago, "For us to love our country, our country must be lovely." The continued loveliness of our country demands that we all dedicate ourselves to a restoration of character. That means demanding more from ourselves and our families, paying attention to what our children are learning in school and from our popular culture, and defending our liberty by getting involved in the political process.

By celebrating character we celebrate the essence of what it means to be American. The Americans we admire most are those who overcome the odds, who persevere despite hardship, who give of themselves to make their neighborhoods and their nations better places to live.

The exemplars of character chronicled in this anthology include presidents, religious leaders, and parents. Their stories are unique, yet they are bound by a common thread best summed up by the famous phrase spoken by one of those celebrated, Winston Churchill: "Never give in, never, never, never, never."

In America today, we glorify many things: wealth, power, fame, athletic ability, and so on. We often ignore the character traits that make these other, more tangible qualities meaningful.

For who among us wants his or her child to admire the wealthy person who becomes so by fraud, the sports champion who cheats or shows poor sportsmanship, or the famous man who is really infamous?

The majority of our citizens believe our country's problems are moral rather than economic. If you spend much time talking with folks around the country, as have I and the authors of *Profiles in Character*, then you know that there is just a general sense of unease in America about the kind of country we're becoming.

Therefore, this celebration of courage couldn't come at a better time.

Nowhere is the loss of character mourned more than in politics. Many Americans question whether their representatives understand their concerns or care about their problems. They are worried that an unhealthy obsession with political power and long careers has replaced true public service.

This volume should provide the skeptics definitive proof that the men and women elected to Congress in November of 1994 understand the people they work for. The people the authors chose to honor demonstrate that this class of freshmen Republicans knows the goodness of America.

Our nation today faces important challenges: balancing the budget by reducing wasteful government spending, reducing taxes, reforming welfare, saving Medicare from bankruptcy, restoring power to parents and city councils and school boards, and improving the standard of living for working families.

Although the authors of these profiles have different ideas about how to solve the many problems that face our nation, they are uniform in the belief that the solutions to our problems will require ample courage from our political leaders. America requires leaders who will keep their promises, who will tell Americans the truth, and who will make the necessary choices to keep America safe, free, and prosperous—for this generation and, more important, for the next. In other words, we will need leaders of exemplary character.

Political character matters so much because freedom is difficult. For nearly thirty years, politicians have preached an ethos of dependency rooted in government from Washington, D.C. Americans were promised security if only they would surrender more of their money, their authority, and their freedom to Washington.

But Americans learned it was a bad bargain. They want their power, their money, and their freedom back. They realized that the only real freedom is freedom with responsibility, that there can be no freedom from responsibility.

The modern welfare state is based on the false belief that freedom from responsibility can work. The tragic circumstances surrounding the poorest Americans prove that it can't.

Only when we reconnect poor people to the world of work, family, and responsibility can we provide real help and real hope.

That's what character is all about. It requires character on the part of politicians to discern between real compassion and false promises, and it requires character on the part of those receiving help because it demands of them a commitment to responsible behavior and self-help.

I'm optimistic about the future of our government because this group of seventy-three Republican freshmen, those whose works appear in this book and their colleagues, consists of people of the finest character. They understand that the solutions to America's problems lie in the hearts and minds of every citizen, not in Washington, D.C. They are men and women who understand that America's best days are yet to come.

I hope these profiles in character will inspire you and remind you of the struggles and tribulations of men and women of character. Honor, faith, duty, perseverance, integrity, commitment to principle, and belief in God sustained them in times of trouble as they sustain us today. We must redouble our efforts to instill these virtues in our fellow citizens and in ourselves, for the future freedom of our republic depends on the continued good character of our people.

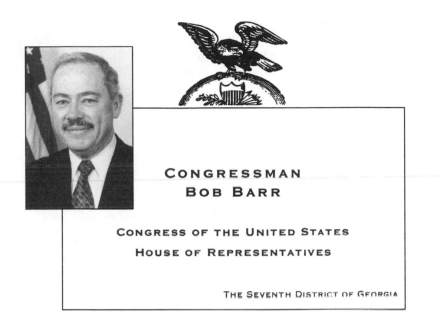

Congressman Barr has an extensive career in government. He served with the Central Intelligence Agency from 1971 to 1978. In 1986, President Reagan appointed Barr United States attorney for the Northern District of Georgia, a position he held until 1990.

Representative Barr received his law degree from Georgetown University and is a member of the Georgia and Florida Bar Associations. He also holds a master's degree in international affairs from George Washington University. Barr is active in several organizations, including Kiwanis, Chamber of Commerce, the National Rifle Association, and the Republican Party. He is a former president of the Southeastern Legal Foundation, a conservative public interest law firm.

Barr is married to the former Jeri Dobbin. They have four children and three grandchildren. The Barrs live in Smyrna, Georgia, northwest of Atlanta. They attend the First United Methodist Church in Marietta.

Congressman Barr's Seventh District covers eleven counties

in western Georgia. He is a member of the Banking and Financial Services, Judiciary, and Veterans Affairs Committees. He is vice-chairman of two of the six subcommittees on which he serves, and chairs the Firearms Legislative Task Force.

How to Contact

1607 Longworth House Office Building,
Washington, D.C. 20515
Telephone: 202-225-2931
Fax: 202-225-2944

BOB BARR

☆ ☆ ☆ ☆ ☆ ☆ ☆ ☆ ☆ ☆ ☆ ☆ ☆ ☆

Shortly after my election to the 104th Congress, I recall reading in *Roll Call*, a Capitol Hill newspaper, that the campaign run against me by the incumbent was considered by political experts to be the second dirtiest campaign in the country that year. Two thoughts immediately came to mind.

The first was to wonder, Who in the world suffered a campaign worse than the one waged against me? I wanted to convey my special condolences.

The second thought was to consider how easy it would be to declare myself yet another victim of the system and wallow in self-pity. I had no trouble fighting off the thought, not only because of the encouragement and support of family and friends throughout the campaign and thereafter, but also because I knew firsthand a public servant who had been the subject of far greater vilification than I and had come through with honor and dignity unscathed. His name is Ed Meese.

I had the pleasure and privilege of serving under Ed Meese during his tenure as attorney general of the United States during President Reagan's second term. I first met with Ed in Washington during the interview process that preceded my nomination by President Reagan to be United States attorney for the Northern District of Georgia. From the first, a friendship was created that I knew would endure.

Great character can be revealed in a variety of ways. I most closely associate two characteristics with Ed Meese. The first is a commitment to core values of honesty and integrity that Ed reflected in his personal conduct toward family and friends in all aspects of his public life. The second characteristic is an unswerving determination to achieve goals regardless of the barriers placed in his way. The barriers, as people who followed his career in Washington know, were many. Ed Meese always knew he had

3

come to our nation's capital to do a job, and he was not going to let the Washington establishment dictate his performance.

Changing the ways of Washington during the 1980s, after years of malaise under the Democrats, was going to take the kind of strong character that Ed brought to town. Well before Reagan's election as president, Ed was known among us conservatives as the Reaganite's Reaganite. As an experienced prosecutor from Alameda County, California, and an expert in the criminal justice system, Ed brought to then Governor Reagan's administration a tough, effective, no-nonsense approach to the crime problem that plagued the nation's most populous state. Among the advisers who formed the nucleus of the California-based policy team for Governor Reagan, Ed was known as the most consistently conservative, as well as the most personable, member of the Reagan team.

Ed brought his conservatism and his engaging personal style to an entrenched Washington that resisted the first and would try to take advantage of the second to defeat it. As one of the three key advisers to the president in the first term, along with Jim Baker and Mike Deaver, Ed demonstrated a canny knack for ensuring that internal White House policy development reflected the president's rather than the staff's views. In a town where even the White House staff often had agendas independent of the boss, that was no small feat. Time and again, especially during budget showdowns, various staffers would caution on the need for compromise. Ed Meese insisted that the president's policies reflected the man in charge; in other words, he wanted to let Reagan be Reagan.

For his efforts on behalf of the president during the first term, Ed was rewarded with an honor he welcomed, to be the president's attorney general. With that honor, however, came an effort to rob him of it. Shortly after his nomination, an independent prosecutor investigated Ed for allegations of ethical misconduct surrounding the efforts by an acquaintance to link government business with a personal friendship. Because of his extremely gracious treatment of people, those opposed to the administration's policies sensed that Ed Meese might be vulnerable, precisely because of his open and gregarious qualities.

The investigation delayed Ed's confirmation for months and revealed no criminal wrongdoing whatsoever. It did reveal how easy it is in Washington to create expensive and time-consuming nuisances for "politically incorrect" public officials. It also wasted an enormous amount of taxpayer dollars and was plainly an effort to defeat the conservative policies of the administration by making an ad hominem attack rather than engaging in substantive debate. This is a political tactic with which I would become only too familiar in my congressional campaign.

Once Ed was confirmed as attorney general, he had ample opportunity to demonstrate his many managerial and legal talents. Whether it was advising the president on judicial appointments or making recommendations to pursue litigation at the appellate or Supreme Court level, Ed was ready with sound legal and policy advice that invariably reflected the views of the president and the millions of Americans who had elected him.

Many people remember Ed for his outstanding role in the Iran-contra investigations. His effort to sort out the matter for the president amid a confusing rash of inconsistent congressional directives still stands as a model exercise of an attorney general giving the president of the United States the kind of expert assistance he deserves from the nation's chief law enforcement official. Although many of Ed's judgment calls were second-guessed in the media and on Capitol Hill, the fact is that they have stood up well over time. The nation would be well served to judge other holders of this important office by his conduct and actions.

As the United States attorney for northern Georgia, I was repeatedly impressed with his ability to know what was going on inside his department and keep his finger on the pulse of the organization. He accomplished this without interfering with the ability of his subordinates to get the job done. Most important, he was always accessible.

An episode from those years with which I was involved and that truly exemplifies Ed's effective management and policy style concerns the prisoner uprising at the federal penitentiary in Atlanta in November 1987. It was a crisis of major proportions for both the country and the Department of Justice. A band of prisoners, many of them detainees from Cuba, had obtained homemade weapons, taken hostages, and set massive fires in the installation.

With the leadership of a very capable FBI team and the careful coordination of decision making with Washington, the episode was successfully concluded without loss of life. As soon as the facility was secure, Ed left Washington and proceeded to Atlanta. No doubt to the dismay of the public relations experts, his first stop was not the pressroom. Rather, he shook hands with and congratulated every line officer who was involved in the effort, thanking all of them profusely for the incredibly successful operation they had just concluded.

When the press sought to tell the story to the public, Ed still refused the limelight. He emphasized instead the local heroes "on the ground" who had executed the operation. The way in which he kept the focus on local officials, rather than on Washington's role, was a textbook example of how a leader builds confidence and morale in an organization. One could not be a part of that event without thinking how impressive Ed Meese was from start to finish.

As the Reagan administration wound down and we returned to the private sector, I was fortunate to have yet another opportunity to work with Ed. He joined the Heritage Foundation in Washington as a Senior Fellow and immediately assisted conservative legal foundations across the country to continue the Reagan Revolution against government overreaching in the courts. I took on the presidency of the Southeastern Legal Foundation at about the same time, so once again the opportunity was there to work with Ed on the issues we both cared about deeply. As always, I found him accessible, helpful, and ready to move our conservative agenda forward.

It was therefore true to form that when I announced my candidacy for elected office, Ed was one of my most enthusiastic supporters. He traveled to Georgia in my behalf and spoke with scores of Georgians about our service together in the Reagan administration. Although campaigning can be tiring, doing so with Ed Meese was always exhilarating. He connected with people as few public officials can do.

When Ed left public office, he wrote about his years with Reagan. The book *With Reagan, the Inside Story* is a fascinating glimpse into the policy deliberations of the Reagan administration. In keeping with Ed's modesty, it is not about Ed Meese, but he was a keen witness and active participant in the key events of Reagan's eight years. Especially impressive are Ed's reflections at the end of the book, published in 1992, that accurately forecasted the issues of the 1994 midterm elections and echoed the sentiments of the vast majority of voters.

To improve the ability of our government to respond to the real needs of the people, Ed recommended a constitutional amendment to provide a line-item veto and also an amendment to provide a balanced budget and tax limitation, requiring on a yearly basis that expenditures not exceed revenues with total taxation and spending limited to a specified percentage of the gross national product.

Ed also called for congressional term limits. Predicting precisely the views of the electorate in 1994, he noted with approval the adoption by several states of congressional term limits. He explained his feeling on the issue by saying, "While I initially had my doubts about this proposal, I see no other way to break the imperious political lifestyle adopted by Congress and to restore the concept of citizen-legislators."

Throughout a long and illustrious career as prosecutor, law school professor, policy and legal adviser to Governor and then President Reagan, and senior spokesman for conservative causes, Ed Meese has demonstrated the qualities that make him one of the great public figures of the latter half of our century. I know that as we approach the twenty-first century, Ed Meese will continue to articulate the principles of limited federal government and personal moral strength that have contributed so much to the successes of conservatism in modern American life.

Ed Meese is truly a profile in character, and I am deeply privileged to call him my friend.

Brownback grew up on the family farm near Parker, Kansas, where he still owns farmland and enjoys helping out with the chores. He and his wife, Mary, have three children, Abby, Andy, and Liz.

Brownback received his bachelor of science, with honors, in agricultural economics from Kansas State University and a law degree from the University of Kansas. He was elected student body president at Kansas State and served as state president and a national officer of the Future Farmers of America.

Following law school he became a partner in a Manhattan, Kansas, law firm and taught agricultural law at Kansas State. Brownback was city attorney for Ogden and Leonardville and served as Riley County Republican Party vice-chairman and Kansas Day Club treasurer.

During 1990–91, Brownback served as a White House Fellow with United States trade representative Carla Hills. He also served on the Intergovernmental Advisory Committee to the United States trade representative.

As secretary of agriculture for the state of Kansas, Congressman Brownback developed innovative programs that saved taxpayers money. He expanded the market for Kansas farm products and led a national marketing effort to use Kansas commodities, such as wheat to produce plastics and animal fat to produce diesel fuel.

Representative Brownback was elected by winning 66 percent of the Second District vote. On the opening day of the 104th Congress, he carried to the floor a reform measure requiring regular audits of Congress by an independent firm, demonstrating his commitment to reduce and reform the federal government. Brownback also has met his pledge to reduce the size of his office staff and is returning 10 percent of his salary to the Treasury. Brownback is following his campaign focus of returning our country to the basic values on which it was built by developing a Family Impact Statement to evaluate the effects of major social legislation on the family structure. Congressman Brownback serves on the Budget, International Relations, and Small Business Committees.

How to Contact

> 1313 Longworth House Office Building,
> Washington, D.C. 20515
> Telephone: 202-225-6601
> Fax: 202-225-2983

☆ ☆ ☆ ☆ ☆ ☆ ☆ ☆ ☆ ☆ ☆ ☆ ☆

A young Englishwoman named Catherine Mumford once wrote an especially pointed letter to William Booth during their courtship, conveying her fear of ambition's powerful influence over men. She saw the seeds of greatness in William, but only if he wisely used the ambition and ability he possessed. She saw everlasting damnation for him if he used his considerable ambition for evil purposes.

In the profoundly insightful letter, Catherine sent to her future husband a warning. She wrote,

> My dearest love, beware how you indulge that dangerous element of character, ambition. Misdirected, it will be everlasting ruin to yourself and, perhaps, to me also. Oh, my love, let nothing earthly excite it, let not self-aggrandizement fire it. Fix it on the Throne of the Eternal, and let it find the realization of its loftiest aspirations in the promotion of His glory, and it shall be consummated with the richest enjoyments and brightest glories of God's own heaven. Those that honor Him, He will honor. And to them who thus see His glory will He give to rule over the nations, and even to judge angels who, through a perverted ambition, the exaltation of self instead of God, have fallen from their allegiance and overcast their eternity with the blackness forever.

Which path would he choose? No one knew William Booth, the founder of the Salvation Army, better than Catherine Mumford. She became not only the mother of his children but also the "mother" of the Salvation Army. In their ministry together, their daily work brought them both dangerously near to ambition's dark side. The temptation to misuse his oratorical gift and fervor for his cause was ever present for Booth. It happened to so many talented men and women.

A gifted minister can move the members of a congregation to

improve themselves, but the lure of power itself is a snare for the overly ambitious. In the beginning, such a man's every thought is only of reaching out to the souls of others, to save the lost for the kingdom of God. The adulation and acclaim frequently bestowed on the successful person may evolve into the self-delusion that the power to change minds resides only within himself. Losing his footing on his solid early path, he begins to seek things more material: a bigger house, better living conditions, money, increased power and influence. Soon the focus is on self instead of others. The source of his energies is no longer God, but himself. When someone reaches that point, failure is sure to follow. As Proverbs 16:18 states, "Pride goes before destruction, and a haughty spirit before a fall."

Would all that happen to William Booth? Catherine plainly saw the risk. She asked what William's ambition would do to him or to her. She later revealed her optimistic leanings and said, "I believe that if God spares him and he is faithful to his trust, his usefulness will be untold, and beyond our capacity to estimate."

William Booth was born on April 10, 1829, in Nottingham, England, the son of Samuel and Mary Booth. Born amid poverty, he had a difficult childhood. When the family went broke, thirteen-year-old William was apprenticed to a pawnbroker. In those days, parents could "rent out" their children to satisfy debts. Not a year later, William was summoned late at night to his parents' bedroom. His father was dying, and he wished to commit his wife and children to the care of God. The somber event launched William's lifelong passion for Christianity. At age fourteen, he demonstrated a depth of understanding rare for any young man; he wanted "to be right with God. I wanted to be right myself. I wanted a life spent in putting other people right."

Booth was a lay minister by age nineteen, and the city of London became his entire world. He became a frequent street preacher, espousing a fiery rhetoric for the Lord, but street preaching paid poorly. He resumed his trade of pawnbroker, though he spent much time preaching. He lived off scant savings and sold his furniture to make ends meet. It was then that he met and fell in love with Catherine Mumford, daughter of a local coach builder and lay Methodist preacher.

Booth was shocked by what he found in the streets of East London. Britain was the richest and most powerful nation on earth, yet the capital city had spawned enormous slums. As machines replaced laboring human hands, the industrial revolution of the nineteenth century took hold. Society had not shifted socially or spiritually to meet the new conditions in the workplace. The situation is comparable to the way our modern society has failed to adequately address the radically different problems caused by America's change from an agricultural and heavy manufacturing economy to one consisting largely of services and high-tech production.

The area of East London where Booth operated was one of the most squalid places on earth. Half a million people were shoehorned into only 290 acres. One impoverished gentleman called it "a great large muck heap, what the rich grows their mushrooms on." Beyond the physical squalor, Booth daily witnessed the enslavement of souls to liquor, promiscuity, and poverty.

Every fifth shop was a gin shop, and many had special arrangements so that even the youngest child could reach the top of the counter. The shops featured a glass of gin for a penny. Smokestacks from factories polluted the air, raw sewage contaminated the historic Thames River, and death and despair were companions to all who lived in East London.

In July 1865, the thirty-six-year-old Booth found his calling to serve the poorest of the poor. After preaching outside the gin mills and bawdy houses, he came home to his wife, Catherine, and proclaimed, "Darling, I have found my destiny!" He would "go for souls." In particular, he would "go for the worst of them!" At first, he tried to bring the unwashed apostates into the regular church community, but he soon discovered there were some members of the congregation not interested in having the local riffraff and ne'er-do-wells seated beside them on Sunday. The poor didn't have nice clothing, and their manners didn't meet the standards of proper etiquette.

So Booth took the church to them. He hired dance halls after the fiddlers had ceased playing. He even preached in haylofts. The system wasn't without problems. During his street preaching, local thugs frequently disrupted his sermons. People hurled eggs at him, and the gin shop owners hired bullies to keep Booth out of their area. It seems his message to the poor was bad for their business. Slowly, souls were saved, and his efforts found roots in the hard heart of East London.

Booth was absolutely convinced that poverty came from a spiritual rather than a mechanistic cause, just as it does today. He rightly observed, "The total transformation of humanity could only be wrought by a subdual of men's will to the will of God." Booth originally created his organization as the Christian Mission to help poor people and those downtrodden in spirit and body. The Christian Mission was one of the five hundred charitable societies operating in East London to assist the poor.

At that time, poor people of East London were not neglected, but they were in danger of being "submerged by the wasteful excesses of sentimental charity," according to Booth. There has been a similar indictment of the welfare system in America today. Booth despised coddling. He was the enemy of every form of softness in dealing with the tribulations of indigent people.

The Christian Mission was continuing its efforts when Booth reviewed the Mission's annual report and statement of purpose, where it was put forth that "the Christian Mission is a volunteer army, recruited from amongst the multitudes who are without God and without hope in the world." Bramwell Booth, William's son and heir apparent to the leadership of the Army, shouted, "A volunteer, I'm no volunteer! I am a regular or nothing." The elder Booth was struck by the expression. He went back to the proof sheets and struck out the word *volunteer*, writing in the word *salvation*. That is how the Salvation Army was conceived. It had all of eighty-eight soldiers to carry on the campaign.

Booth would create an army of salvationists whose aim was to win souls to God. He was selected its first general, and like a commander, he was fundamentally autocratic. The Army set up shelters and food depots in 1880 that were besieged by the crowds. In 1889, the Salvation Army provided homeless people in London 192 tons of bread and 140 tons of potatoes.

About the same time Booth wrote his epic book, *In Darkest England and the Way Out*. It was a plan for bringing poor people of England out from under the dual poverty of spirit and body. Within four months of the book's appearance, Booth had enough funds to establish food depots, shelters, and labor bureaus. There was to be no coddling or softness. People were to work for their food and a roof over their heads. They were to receive training and support, but mostly, they were to receive nurturing for the soul. Indeed, Booth was to write gleefully in his diary, "Souls! Souls! Souls! My heart hungers for souls."

General William Booth made his last public appearance on May 9, 1912, in the Royal Albert Hall in London. It was the celebration of his eighty-third birthday. He was physically fragile and almost blind, but his mind was not diminished by time. He mesmerized the audience with these closing words: "While women weep, as they do now, I'll fight; while men go to prison, in and out, as they do now, I'll fight; while there is a drunkard left, while there is a poor lost girl upon the streets, while there remains one dark soul without the light of God, I'll fight; I'll fight to the very end!"

William Booth died at his home on August 20, 1912, but his

fight to alleviate the suffering of poor people continues through the soldiers of the Salvation Army. He spawned a global organization that today brings comfort and God's love to more than one hundred countries. Worldwide, the Salvation Army has two million soldiers who give new meaning to the word *dedicated*. The Army distributes food and provides shelter to more than nine million people in the United States alone each year.

The Army's emphasis is first on the soul and its transition, but the soldiers recognize that it's tough to absorb God's message on an empty stomach. Though he was an Englishman, William Booth's methods were born in America. American revivalists preaching in England stirred the passions of young William and Catherine Booth. The British clergy, as Booth came to see them, had been robbed of any trace of holy fire by years of formal, restrained training. American firebrands such as Caughey, Palmer, and Charles Finney made a deep impression on the founders of the Salvation Army as early as the 1840s. In those champions of the faith, Booth saw ambition that saved souls instead of corrupting them.

Following their lead, Booth became a spellbinding preacher and tremendous motivator. He could articulate his visions in ways that made people want to pick up his banner and march! As a visionary, Booth is part of the history of English religious radicalism, a line of descent that includes William Blake, a prominent English poet, painter, engraver, and mystic. Blake had a vivid faith in the unseen, and he was guided, he believed, by visitation from the spiritual world. Blake died in 1827, two years before William Booth was born. As with Blake, there is a growing recognition of Booth's cultural significance as a visionary—Blake as an equal of Shakespeare and Booth as an equal of Augustine or Martin Luther. That means equality not as a theologian, but as a personal example of applied theology, the essence of thought and soul in action.

Booth was passionate in personality and peaceful in vision. He struggled inwardly with a nature that was at odds with itself. He was a loving yet unsparing man; generous yet rigorous; warmhearted yet demanding. The seemingly opposite extremes stirred his character, making him mercurial and emotional, given to undue elation and deep despair. He was a man with enough innate ambition, drive, and passion to accomplish great things.

Booth displayed an essential American character trait, ambition. It is simultaneously a very real blessing and a very real danger. Ambition is a blessing that when used rightfully can lead to accomplishments of service and contribution. Used selfishly, it will take a man on a downward slide to personal destruction. In our century, there are examples of dangerous and blessed ambitions. Adolf Hitler's dangerous and unchecked ambition resulted in World War II. Martin Luther King, Jr., was also ambitious, but we take courage and inspiration from the selfless vision of a color-blind society he gave to our nation.

As one writer has stated of ambition, "It is healthy only when it is used *with others,* not at the *expense of others.* Ambition is most mature when we understand what we possess and how to give it. It is most meaningful and virtuous when it is for the benefit of others." How did Booth successfully battle the potential dangers of his ambition? Why did he not succumb to the same pressures that drive others toward self-aggrandizement and self-gratification?

Booth's secret in taming his ambition was recognizing the source of his power. He was not the lightning bolt that would accomplish great things through the Salvation Army. It was God. He acknowledged, as the modern evangelist Luis Palau concedes, "that the whole thing is not I, but Christ, in me. It's not what I am going to do for you, but rather what you're going to do through me." Booth well knew where his strength originated.

The Old Testament story of the burning bush in the wilderness is known to many people. The prophet Moses saw a bush burning in the wilderness without a source for its flame. It continued to burn and burn, but was never consumed. God had placed His hand on the bush, causing its miraculous fire, while telling Moses to return to Pharaoh and demand the release of the enslaved Jewish people. That burning bush was in William Booth and is in each one of us. Each of us possesses a body God can work through if we will allow Him. With God, we are an incredible fire that burns bright, illuminating a world for all to see.

William Booth had God's fire in his belly. He observed that "man can no more leave God out of his philosophies than he can live without his heart or see without his eyes." The only way Booth could control the danger of runaway ambition was to completely focus on God. He had done that since his youth. At age fifteen, Booth made a commitment that "God shall have all there is of William Booth." He never strayed from that commitment.

At the pinnacle of his career Booth was consulted by kings. He knew they were not consulting William Booth, even though he was mouthing the words; rather, the spirit of God flowed through him. Booth never lost sight of his objective. When he visited King Edward VII, he wrote in the king's album, "Some men's ambition is art. Some men's ambition is fame. Some men's ambition is gold. My ambition is the souls of men."

I am a member of the 104th Congress, and the dangerous side of personal ambition is always present. It searches for moments of weakness when I might succumb to the desire for personal fame rather than service to God and my fellow human beings. It happens all too often in me, yet I look at the life of William Booth and draw strength in my beliefs. I know that if I remain true to my God and focus on His Word, Catherine Booth's prediction of what would happen in William's life will be true, at least to a small degree, in mine.

Catherine rightly prophesied, "I believe that if God spares him, *and he is faithful to his trust*, his usefulness will be untold, and beyond our capacity to estimate."

I pray that you will be faithful to your trust so that you may be useful to your family and your nation, and your capacity for good shall be inestimable.

CONGRESSMAN
ED BRYANT

CONGRESS OF THE UNITED STATES
HOUSE OF REPRESENTATIVES

THE SEVENTH DISTRICT OF TENNESSEE

A native of west Tennessee, Representative Bryant attended the University of Mississippi for both undergraduate and law school. He graduated in 1970 with a B.A. in history and obtained the J.D. law degree in 1972. In 1970, Bryant was commissioned an army officer through the ROTC and served in the Military Intelligence branch. He was later chosen to join the Judge Advocate General's Corps. From 1977 to 1978, he taught future officers at the United States Military Academy at West Point, New York.

Congressman Bryant is a former president of the Madison County Bar Association, and he served on the boards of the Rotary Club, Little League, and Fellowship of Christian Athletes. He is a long-standing member of the Tennessee Farm Bureau. Bryant served as United States attorney for the Western District of Tennessee following appointment by President George Bush. He headed an office of twenty-nine attorneys and led the prosecution of the nation's first civil rights case of sexual harassment against a sitting judge. His office ranked among the top offices nationally in the prosecution of violent criminals and was one of the first United States attorneys to investigate fraud in the health care system.

Bryant is married to the former Cyndi Lemons, and they have three sons: Matt, Josh, and Drew.

Congressman Bryant represents a unique fifteen-county district extending from the eastern suburbs of Memphis to the Kentucky border in middle Tennessee. He has been appointed to the House Task Force on Firearms, formed by House Speaker Gingrich to address a wide range of gun issues. Bryant is cochairman of the Family Caucus and serves on the Leaders Task Force on Legal Reform and on the Agriculture and Judiciary Committees. Subcommittees include Crime and Immigration, Department Operations, and Specialty Crops.

How to Contact

> 1516 Longworth House Office Building,
> Washington, D.C. 20515
> Telephone: 202-225-2811
> Fax: 202-225-2989

☆ ☆ ☆ ☆ ☆ ☆ ☆ ☆ ☆ ☆ ☆ ☆ ☆

I first heard of Elizabeth Newton when I was well beyond my college years and history studies. Possessing an abiding faith in God and much determination, Elizabeth taught her son John to read by the time he was three. Under her tutelage, he memorized Bible verses and learned to read Latin. Her desire was for him to enter the ministry. No doubt she prayed diligently for him. She died in 1732 when John was only seven years old.

Though Newton would later confess that he had wasted all of the loving advantages provided by his mother, her persistent efforts would eventually take root. At the innocent age of eleven John was taken to sea by his father, a ship's captain, to begin his maritime career. By his early adult behavior and the manner in which he earned his living, his associates could not imagine he came from such a purist background.

John Newton became the hated captain of a slave-trading ship. So despised was he that when he once fell overboard in a drunken stupor, the crew actually harpooned him in the leg to rescue him. As a result of that injury, he limped for the rest of his life. There would follow years of debauchery and harrowing experiences, including brushes with death and disease.

John struggled with his terrible existence. The words of his mother, from a childhood long ago, never left him. His training was like a planted seed, nurtured with prayer by the patient Elizabeth Newton. By the amazing grace of God, the seed that was sown fell not on unyielding rock but on fertile soil. Elizabeth's son finally received his salvation and surrendered to the grace of a loving and forgiving God.

In 1779, John Newton wrote one of the most popular and emotionally charged hymns to ever reverberate through a sanctuary. It is my favorite, and I can never hear "Amazing Grace" without thinking about that faithful and persistent mother.

I would like to share with you these wonderful words:

Amazing grace, how sweet the sound,
That saved a wretch like me!
I once was lost, but now am found,
Was blind, but now I see.

'Twas grace that taught my heart to fear,
And grace my fears relieved;
How precious did that grace appear,
The hour I first believed!

Through many dangers, toils, and snares,
I have already come;
'Tis grace hath brought me safe thus far,
And grace will lead me home.

When we've been there ten thousand years,
Bright shining as the sun;
We've no less days to sing God's praise,
Than when we'd first begun.

Little did Elizabeth Newton know what God had in store for her young son or how his song, and many others he would write, would enormously affect other lives over the next two centuries. She knew few conveniences, suffered sparse encouragement from a seafaring husband, and endured disabling bouts with a disease that would eventually kill her. And yet, she sowed the seeds of character in young John and interceded in his behalf with prayer. They were prayers that saw not an immediate response, but in God's perfect time, they reaped a bountiful crop.

I know with certainty that there is a unique bond between a boy and his mother. It is through the living example of mothers like Elizabeth Newton that we learn how to produce a legacy to the world that has eternal value.

An interesting story I always remember when discussing parental responsibilities concerns the year 1809.* If in that day there had been evening news, it would have focused on the military adventures of the French general Napoleon Bonaparte. (CNN would have been broadcasting live from the battlefields of Europe!) In that same year, quietly and without notice, babies were being born. That is not a particularly newsworthy situation, except that 1809 was a very good year for babies.

Among them were future President Abraham Lincoln, writer Edgar Allan Poe, naturalist Charles Darwin, inventor Cyrus McCormick, frontiersman Kit Carson, poets Alfred, Lord Tennyson and Oliver Wendell Holmes, Sr., British Prime Minister William Gladstone, and composer Felix Mendelssohn. The men would achieve historical significance in a wide range of arenas, and many would have far greater impact on the world than Napoleon had. Yet such events as their births and early years were, for most of them, unreported. What is important is the role each mother played in shaping the character of her son.

The more portentous that current politics and events become, the higher the priorities parents must establish to instill the seeds of strong character in their children. The need is here. The need is now. In today's homes are the future presidents, writers, and scientists whose decisions and discoveries will transform the world.

Over the years, I have learned to appreciate what I believe to be a very special bond that exists between mothers and sons. I am certainly the beneficiary of such a relationship with my mother, who is nearing her eighty-ninth birthday. My brother and I were raised by this godly woman, strongly committed to all the good things and moral values of her generation. Being the oldest daughter among eleven children, she helped her own mother raise the younger siblings.

Without doubt, this experience was invaluable when my

brother and I came along. She stayed home with me until I began the first grade, then she returned to the demanding work of a nurse at a hospital. She wisely chose scheduling on the night shift to be home with me during the idle times of school afternoons and the long days of summer when an ungoverned child might stray in the wrong direction.

Looking back on the many good memories of those growing-up years, I recall a steadying influence, a quiet mother who loved me and who instilled the character points in my life that still motivate me and hold me accountable. To this day, she holds firm in her confidence of me and continues to be a source of wisdom and inspiration.

At this moment, the wonderful mother of my children and I are approaching our twenty-fifth wedding anniversary. I marvel at how Cyndi's love for our three sons is so much like my own mother's love for me. Our boys are now twenty-two, eighteen, and fourteen. There are more stress and turmoil in their lives, and the mother-son relationship is more difficult to maintain. It seems to be about the time of junior high school, the age of discovery (of girls and cars and video games), when boys begin their awkward and inevitable journey toward personal independence. More often, a mother carries the spiritual burdens for the sons, and she never ceases loving and praying for them, just as mine does.

I know of Cyndi's concern for our sons' well-being, her patience in time of trial, her looking for the best in them, and her diligence in lifting them (and me) up in prayer. Even when Dad loses his patience, Mother stands by them. It is doubtful our boys appreciate or even understand this positive force at work in their lives, but like me with my mother, I trust that they will come to recognize and cherish it as they mature.

In the fast-paced world of today, whether the traditional family or the single-parent version, with one income or two, I can sit back and think about the wonderful potential a mother possesses to bring good into the lives of her children. It is surely not by accident that mothers seem to lay a special claim to Proverbs 22:6: "Train up a child in the way he should go, and when he is old he will not depart from it."

I am truly thankful that I have two godly mothers in my life. My sons and I are, indeed, blessed.

---

*Source unknown.

CONGRESSMAN
STEVE CHABOT

CONGRESS OF THE UNITED STATES
HOUSE OF REPRESENTATIVES

THE FIRST DISTRICT OF OHIO

A resident of Cincinnati, Representative Chabot is a native of the Queen City and a graduate of LaSalle High School. After graduating from the College of William and Mary, he returned to Cincinnati and taught elementary school during the day and attended the Salmon P. Chase College of Law at night. Upon obtaining his law degree, Chabot opened his own neighborhood law practice.

Congressman Chabot was elected to the Cincinnati City Council in 1985, where he served until 1990 when he was appointed to the Hamilton County Board of Commissioners. He subsequently won public election to the Board, serving until his election to Congress in 1994. Chabot lives in the Westwood neighborhood of Cincinnati with his wife, Donna, daughter, Erica, and son, Randy.

Chabot is well known in Cincinnati for his innovative approaches to welfare and crime issues. While serving in local government, he won the right to jail criminals two to a cell, and put nonviolent prisoners to work on public projects. He also launched a program to give welfare recipients the opportunity to work by turning abandoned buildings into useful housing stock.

Congressman Chabot's First District encompasses most of Cincinnati and its western suburbs. He was elected in 1994 by a twelve-point margin. Congressman Chabot has become one of Congress's leading balanced budget advocates, voting repeatedly to shrink the federal government and reduce wasteful spending. He has been an outspoken defender of citizens' privacy rights. He fielded a bipartisan coalition to oppose the "1-800-Big Brother" provision of the House immigration bill, a sweeping assertion of federal power that would have forbidden any new employee to work without first getting the express approval of the federal government. Chabot serves on the Judiciary, International Relations, and Small Business Committees and on five subcommittees.

How to Contact

1641 Longworth House Office Building, Washington, D.C. 20515
Telephone: 202-225-2216
Fax: 202-225-3012

☆ ☆ ☆ ☆ ☆ ☆ ☆ ☆ ☆ ☆ ☆ ☆ ☆ ☆

Civic virtue. To me, these words are embodied in the man who has been an inspiration throughout my career. He is Eugene Ruehlmann, former mayor of Cincinnati, who, like the Roman farmer after whom our city is named, has been willing to sacrifice private interests when his community needed him most. In his family life, in charitable work, and in public office, Gene Ruehlmann exemplifies the virtues that have made our nation great and upon which a civil society depends.

I know it may not be politically correct for a congressional reformer to devote a chapter in this book to someone who has given large portions of his life to public service. My staff has reminded me that it may be imprudent to extol the virtues of a politician when there are so many nonpolitical heroes in Cincinnati from whom to choose. The simple explanation is that aside from my immediate family, Gene Ruehlmann has influenced me as no one else has done. Time and again, he has proven how one person can be a force for good and make a noticeable difference in the lives of others.

While people in Washington, D.C., may scoff at the notion, folks in Cincinnati will understand immediately how this former mayor and party leader represents the best in American political society. Through his unending personal commitment to the well-being of our community, Gene Ruehlmann has changed Cincinnati and strengthened our institutions. Over the past five decades, at critical points in our city's history, he has stepped forward to lead with quiet example and hard work. He is at once a strong political partisan and a unifying force. Repeatedly, he has brought people together in causes that have ranged from calming racial tensions to revitalizing a once decaying central city, while reforming a county political organization that had been ravaged by scandal and arrogance.

The example of integrity in office that I observed set by Gene

Ruehlmann motivated my entry into local politics in the post-Watergate era. In the late 1970s, national politics had a bad reputation; but locally, Gene had shown the good that a committed public servant could accomplish. Born in the same Price Hill neighborhood where I grew up, Gene had been an icon of public service on the Cincinnati City Council throughout my youth. I was a student at LaSalle High School when he was mayor during the turbulent late sixties. He was a rock of stability and civility that all could see, not like the shadowy figures I saw on television during the Watergate investigation of my college years. Gene set the standard of what I thought a public servant's potential to serve the common good could be.

By the time I first ran for City Council, unsuccessfully and as an independent, Gene had withdrawn from public life. I was especially gratified when he played a major role in encouraging me to run a second time, as a Republican. My wife, Donna, happened to be the hygienist for Gene's dentist, and she can be as relentless in her personal style of campaigning as Gene or I have ever been. Of course, that is not to suggest that Gene would ever be influenced by a dental assistant peering into his mouth while wielding a sharp instrument.

Gene returned to public life in 1991, answering the call of a besieged and scandal-torn Hamilton County Republican Party to serve as its chairperson. I had just made the move from City Council to become a Hamilton County commissioner, replacing a Republican who had crashed his county-owned vehicle while driving the wrong way on Interstate 275. In addition, my predecessor's uncle had recently resigned as county auditor amidst accusations of granting favorable tax treatment to political cronies. It was painfully clear that our county party needed an overhaul. It needed the integrity that Gene's leadership could provide, and it needed the public trust that the former mayor's reputation could help restore to our citizens.

Not many people really wanted to be the heir to such responsibility, but after a twenty-year hiatus from public affairs, "Clean
Gene" stepped in and lent his considerable authority to remaking
the dominant political party in southern Ohio. He undertook the
task simply because he believed it was the right thing to do. Once
again, his commitment to excellence in government had a tremendous positive influence on my life. He worked to create a healthy
civic environment in which a new county officeholder could
accomplish meaningful changes.

I am sure that Gene Ruehlmann's devotion to public affairs
and civic virtue will be as inspirational to others as it has been to
me. He worries that the concept of public service has again
slipped into disrepute. His entire life is a testament to the good
that public service can accomplish. His story is remarkable, yet
deeply rooted in traditional American values that reach back to
our nation's founders. It is a further reflection of Gene's character
that he shies away from having his life recounted. There are
Cincinnatians far more deserving than he is, he has protested.
"And there are a lot of things that I could have done and should
have done that have not been accomplished." Perhaps. But I
believe the five-decade span of Gene Ruehlmann's public service
is worthy of celebration.

Eugene P. Ruehlmann was born to the children of German
immigrants seventy years ago in Cincinnati, Ohio. The ninth of
ten children, he knows of what he speaks when he preaches that
"a strong family is the most important element of society today."
Ask him how long he has been married to his lovely wife, Virginia, and he will answer to the day (forty-eight years, nine
months, nine days, and counting, as I write). He glows with pride
when he speaks of his eight children and twenty-one grandchildren, proudly noting that each of his offspring has earned at least
a college degree. That level of education was not available to
Gene's father who, without the benefit of finishing high school,

went from being a salesman of burial insurance policies to being a vice president of a Cincinnati-based major insurance company.

Gene credits his parents with instilling in him a deep religious faith, a strong work ethic, and a tight family bond that has kept the large Ruehlmann clan closely entwined. He fondly recalls his mother, a woman of profound faith, reading nightly from a huge Bible in her bedroom. To this day, Gene and his wife attend church every Sunday, and Gene is not afraid to make public his affirmation of the blessings God has given him. His faith is an integral part of his life.

Gene's mother and father emphasized to their children the importance of education. Gene graduated from the University of Cincinnati, as did Virginia, who was chosen the outstanding woman in her class. After graduating with honors from Harvard Law School, Gene returned to the Queen City, living first in Price Hill and then moving his family to Delhi Township. As he and Virginia raised their family, he also helped build a prominent law firm. Gene practiced law for nine years before running for a part-time seat on the City Council in 1959. Unlike me, he won his first time on the ballot.

The City Council on which he served and which he led as mayor from 1967 to 1971 is remembered favorably in Cincinnati. His administration ushered in what I have referred to as something of a golden age of Cincinnati politics. Gene joined such lions as Bill Gradison, Charlie Taft, Bill Keating, and Democratic governor-to-be John Gilligan on a City Council that frequently was able to put the public interest ahead of partisan advantage. Gene credits others with what the council was able to accomplish, and that innate modesty helps explain his effectiveness.

Working alongside business and political leaders, community activists, and private developers, Gene and his colleagues helped revitalize Cincinnati's faltering central business district. They fashioned a comprehensive development plan that shaped the city we know today. Most notably, they were instrumental in clearing unsightly dilapidated buildings from the historic Fountain Square area that has now been reborn and provides so much charm, character, and pleasure to our residents. Taking things one step at a time and keeping his expectations high but realistic, Gene led the way in a downtown redevelopment that saw a new convention center rise, created a boom in office building construction, and encouraged innovations such as Cincinnati's unique second-level "skywalk" system. It was truly an era of local government at its best.

Gene's tenacity was especially apparent in his battle to bring major league football to Cincinnati, and keep the Cincinnati Reds baseball team in town, by convincing the city to build a new sports stadium. Historic Crosley Field was just not up to the task, the owner of the Reds was being courted by interests from San Diego, and the promise of the newly consolidated National Football League was beckoning. Gene wryly recounts that "getting the new stadium built was like running an obstacle course." At a critical moment in the planning phase, for example, the city cut off funds needed for development of stadium specifications. Gene went to the private sector, and in a marathon fund-raising tour de force, he raised the necessary $250,000 within the narrow ten-day window he was given.

Paul Brown, having been fired by Cleveland Browns owner Art Modell, was amenable to starting a new professional football franchise in Cincinnati. Gene helped work out the terms by bringing together the many decision-making factions. In 1967, newly appointed NFL Commissioner Pete Rozelle called Gene on the telephone and made a verbal commitment to Cincinnati. Based on that promise, the council proceeded with bond issues to finance stadium construction. It was a different era.

Gene Ruehlmann scrambled to solve one problem after another. Lawsuits by dissenters were filed and overcome. Business leaders balked at their previous commitment and then re-grouped. When Reds owner Bill DeWitt hesitated to sign the new stadium lease, Gene prevailed upon him to sell the team to a hometown group of investors committed to keeping the Big Red Machine in our city. Remarkably, the city and county governments that were frequently at odds came together as one. Paul Brown's Bengals football team played at the University of Cincinnati stadium in 1968 and 1969. By 1970, they were able to move into the all new Riverfront Stadium, inaugurated by the Reds' first game in June.

Some issues never die. Now, a quarter century later, the voters have passed a sales tax increase to provide for two new stadiums. But Gene's ceaseless and untiring efforts to make Riverfront Stadium a reality still provide a textbook civic lesson of great value to anyone in local government who must unite diverse interests to accomplish a monumental task.

Undoubtedly, the most formidable challenge in his public life confronted Gene as he became mayor, shortly after the stadium deal was struck. Racial tensions were running high when Gene took over in December 1967. Riots had ripped at the heart of the city just months before. Once again, Gene's integrity and ability to bring disparate people together, coupled with his fundamental decency, served the community extremely well.

As is so often the case, very real problems had been exacerbated by a failure of communication. Gene reached out to segments of the community that government officials had neglected. Without fanfare and without seeking to garner personal attention in the press, he worked to open lines of discussion between Cincinnatians of all races. Gene helped establish a new Human Relations Commission; he walked the streets and talked with citizens; he and his wife worshiped in black churches across the city. For the first time, meaningful communication developed between city hall and leaders of the African-American community. Meanwhile, increasing downtown development provided a source of job opportunities and hope for the future.

Gene Ruehlmann's spirit of inclusion, his vigorous outreach, his unassuming personal style, his civility in the face of adversity, his deep commitment to antidiscrimination and equality before the law, all set a standard that Cincinnatians would do well to remember today.

In 1971, with progress made on many fronts, Gene Ruehlmann surrendered the yearly salary of $11,500 that he had received for the seventy-hour-a-week "part-time" mayor's job. He returned to the full-time practice of law. It was an easily understood decision for a man with eight college-bound children. An enjoyable retirement from public life was certainly well deserved. But twenty years later, when his party called him again, he returned to the political fray. "I'm always looking for new mountains to climb," he replied when asked why he would step into the county Republican Party chairmanship under adverse circumstances. Virginia acknowledges that Gene is a mountain climber, but she notes that he did not necessarily have to pick Mount Everest. That is an appropriate description of the mountain of problems he inherited. The party, quite frankly, very much needed the reforms he urged it to take.

Political organizations are not always capable of initiating internal reform, but Gene has been up to the challenge. He has been rigorous in demanding that publicly elected officials give the taxpayers a high level of job performance and that they insist upon the same high standards for their staffs. He has brought long overdue reforms that prevent government employees from being coerced into contributing to campaign funds. By enforcing the highest standards of integrity within the county party, he has rendered a great service to the community as a whole. The "Clean Gene" nickname awarded him by the press decades ago, which he typically calls "a lot of garbage," is still an accurate moniker and reflects the character of the man.

Just as Gene's public works and his family have blessed and strengthened our community, so have his private charitable endeavors. His work on behalf of the United Way and various local hospitals is legendary, and he has raised millions for these deserving causes. He continues to serve on charitable boards, including the board of directors of Children's Hospital and the Work Rehabilitation Center, which provides meaningful assistance to disabled working men and women. The list of significant charitable projects to which Gene has lent his time and energies over the years is too lengthy to recount.

Gene Ruehlmann has been a friend and an inspiration not only to me but also to many, many other people across Cincinnati. He has made a profound difference to our community. Gene is fond of reciting the Athenian oath, which states, "We will transmit this nation, not less but greater, better and more beautiful than it was transmitted to us." Gene Ruehlmann certainly does his duty to serve that end, and he brings honor to the words *public service.*

**CONGRESSWOMAN
HELEN CHENOWETH**

CONGRESS OF THE UNITED STATES
HOUSE OF REPRESENTATIVES

THE FIRST DISTRICT OF IDAHO

Born in eastern Kansas, Representative Chenoweth spent her early years in the farming community of Burlingame. During World War II, the family moved to California. After the war the family moved to Grant's Pass, Oregon, where they returned to their agricultural roots.

Chenoweth attended Whitworth College in Spokane, Washington, and moved to Idaho in 1964. From 1964 to 1975, she was a medical and legal management consultant with a national client following. In that role, she recruited physicians from medical schools across the nation to serve in Northwest towns and clinics.

Chenoweth has been a guest instructor at the University of Idaho's School of Law. From 1975 to 1977, she was state executive director of the Idaho Republican Party.

She served as chief of staff to Congressman Steve Symms, and after leaving that office in 1978, she founded Consulting Associates, Inc. The firm specialized in issues relating to natural resources, energy, and environmental policy; government contracts; and political management. Representative Chenoweth is a nationally recognized spokesperson for private property rights.

Chenoweth is a member of the Resources and Agriculture Committees and serves on five subcommittees.

How to Contact

> 1722 Longworth House Office Building, Washington, D. C. 20515
> Telephone: 202-225-6611

☆ ☆ ☆ ☆ ☆ ☆ ☆ ☆ ☆ ☆ ☆ ☆ ☆ ☆

I t was the French Revolution of 1848, and smoke choked the barricaded streets of Paris. Angry mobs shouted, "Bread or blood!" Blood had indeed been spilled, for clattering down one street was a wagon piled high with bodies, while young revolutionaries called to the people to gaze upon the work of the National Guard.

Since the earlier revolution of 1789, France had suffered from many periods of disturbance and political calamity, separated by the narrow gulfs between incompetent or corrupt governments. Once again, the failure of the laws and institutions to be just had driven people to violence. It had been a depressingly familiar scene in France since the overthrow of Louis XVI, who was guillotined for "acts of treason" in 1793. France had pursued a disastrous series of failed governments. The First Republic accommodated the rise of Napoleon Bonaparte, who became emperor in 1804; Napoleon I's failure in war in 1814 brought the House of Bourbon back to the throne with Louis XVIII, who was succeeded by his brother, Charles X. He, in turn, lasted only six years until he was deposed by the revolution of 1830.

Many French politicians claimed the nation was finally pursuing middle-class democracy under Louis Philippe, "the citizen king." Instead, France got an incestuous monarchy that rewarded political connections and impeded the activities of the marketplace, bringing depression and poverty to the French people.

The social and political failures of this period reached a revolutionary climax in 1848 that would see the rise, and then the collapse, of a corrupt democracy and the eventual coronation of a new emperor. George Roach, educator, historian, and president of Hillsdale College, observed that "political interventions, combining the abuses of a past monarchy and a present democracy, had combined to undermine the prosperity and the morality of the French people, leaving them without principle and without a leader, rudderless in the midst of a revolutionary storm that had not yet seen a lasting end."

In those years of upheaval and confusion emerged a voice of common sense and clarity of thought. The voice belonged to an unlikely hero, a pale, sickly, and bookish country squire named Frederic Bastiat. Although not a gifted speaker, Bastiat possessed a powerful intellect and a slicing wit. He was an engaging conversationalist and gifted writer. During his short life, and the even shorter life he strode upon the public stage, Bastiat provided some of the most incisive commentary ever voiced about the nature of freedom and the proper role of government in guaranteeing that freedom for its people.

Doubtless, Bastiat would find it humorously ironic that the lessons he struggled so valiantly to teach his countrymen would, a century and a half later, inspire modern Americans who are facing many of the same internal problems that faced a revolutionary France. Frederic Bastiat was born in 1801 in the town of Bayonne near the beautiful Bay of Biscay in southern France. His father was a respected merchant who owned a small estate. By Frederic's tenth birthday, both of his parents had died, and he was being raised by his grandfather and a maiden aunt. Early prospects for the young man hinted toward a comfortable life, but he showed no signs of greatness.

Before his death, Frederic's father had remarked that the young Bastiat "is as good as he is lazy. If he is going to do something in life, he is going to have to change radically. Frederic is always pleasant and good natured; but he has a lazy streak that is without equal. What a shame that I don't have the means to give him the education he deserves." Nonetheless, Bastiat was able to attend respectable schools where he developed fluency in English and a fascination with economics, for which he is well known. He was especially interested in the economic theories espoused by Adam Smith, a Scottish economist and philosopher, and Thomas

Malthus, an English economist and clergyman. After leaving school, Bastiat retired to his family's country estate and spent the next twenty years looking after the affairs of the farm and continuing his intellectual pursuits in virtual obscurity.

Bastiat dabbled in regional politics and corresponded regularly with other politicians and scholars. Still, throughout the years of turmoil that saw the rise and fall of Louis XVIII and Charles X, and the ascension of Louis Philippe, he remained a little-known country gentleman who only occasionally published his thoughts concerning free trade. According to George Roach, "these were years during which France was sliding into a morass of socialism. But that course of events had not yet become clear to Bastiat and France."

Almost by accident, Bastiat made a discovery that was to change the last decade of his life and make him one of the leading figures of political and economic thought. To settle a point on an insult the British prime minister had been accused of directing at France, Bastiat began researching English newspapers to find the original text of the speech. In so doing, he discovered that a vibrant free trade movement had emerged in England. The unexpected find of an energetic political movement of like-minded people across the Channel energized Bastiat.

He immediately took up a lively correspondence with one of the movement's leaders, Richard Cobden, who preached free trade and government nonintervention in commerce. His communications with Cobden and his growing involvement with the French free trade movement finally inspired Bastiat to submit an essay to the most prestigious French economic journal of his day, *Journal des economistes*. His essay, an ambitious study of the effects of English and French tariffs on economic growth, was published in October 1844.

Today it is hard to appreciate how a single essay on economics could have the effect that Bastiat's did. Among the journal's editors and its erudite audience, at the age of forty-three, Frederic Bastiat had emerged as an overnight sensation. Complimentary letters from across France began arriving at his country home. Less than a year later Bastiat visited Paris to make arrangements for publishing a book on Cobden and the free trade movement in England. He came away with the offer to become editor of the *Journal des economistes,* and the suggestion he could assume a chair at a university.

Bastiat had entered the most productive period of his life. He generated commentary and analysis for the increasing number of newspapers and journals that had taken up the economic debate. The debate was of profound general interest because although France was becoming more industrialized, with one-seventh of its workers laboring in the growing industrial base, the national economy was burdened by impediments to trade imposed by the government. The impediments manifested themselves in a disastrous human toll; in the city of Lyon, 100,000 of the 150,000 residents were described as indigent, and there were an estimated 130,000 abandoned children living in the streets of French cities.

Such privation enraged Bastiat, who was struck by the inconsistencies between what the government claimed to be doing for the people and the real-world effects on their lives. A collection of his articles, entitled *Economic Sophisms,* was published in 1845 and recorded the following scene:

> I enter one of the cottages that cling to the French side of the Pyrenees. The head of the family receives only a slender wage for his work. His half-naked children shiver in the icy north wind; the fire is out and there is nothing on the table. On the other side of the mountain there are wool, firewood and corn; but these goods are forbidden to the family of the poor day laborer, for the other side of the mountain is not in France. Foreign spruce will not gladden the hearth; the shepherd's children will not know the taste of Biscayean maslin; and wool from Navarre will never warm their numbed

limbs. All this is, we are told, in the interest of the general welfare. Very well, but then it must be admitted that in this instance the general welfare is in conflict with justice.

How often today do we see programs touted as being in the interest of the "general welfare" that are, in fact, counterproductive or unjust?

Despite the bitterness he felt over the failure of government policy, to his credit, Bastiat was able to use humor and satire with cutting effectiveness to ridicule the specious arguments against free market economics. In the *Courier Français* on September 18, 1846, he wrote a facetious essay calling for a law to be passed requiring that all labor be performed with the left hand only. He sarcastically rationalized his idea by saying, "The old system of restriction was based on the idea of creating obstacles in order to multiply job opportunities. The new system of restriction that we are proposing to take its place is based on exactly the same idea."

Bastiat continued, "Since it is so much more difficult to work with the left hand than the right, imagine, Sire, the immense number of people that will be needed to meet the present demand for consumers' goods. So prodigious a demand for manual labor cannot fail to bring about a considerable rise in wages, and pauperism will disappear from the country as if by magic."

By the fall of 1846, Bastiat's Free Trade Association was holding meetings and discussions that drew crowds as large as two thousand, a considerable assemblage in that day. To lead the effort more effectively, Bastiat left his beloved estate for Paris. There, he assumed the editorship of a new free trade newspaper published by his association, *Le Libre-échange*. Many of Bastiat's best pieces appeared in the journal, including his most famous satire, the *Petition of the Candlemakers:*

From:

The Manufacturers of Candles, Tapers, Lanterns, Candlesticks, Street Lamps, Snuffers and Extinguishers; and from the producers of Tallow, Oil, Resin, Alcohol, and Generally of Everything Connected with Lighting.

To:

The Honorable Members of the Chamber of Deputies.

Gentlemen:

We are suffering from ruinous competition of a foreign rival who apparently works under conditions so far superior to our own for the production of light that he is *flooding the domestic market* with it at an incredibly low price; for the moment he appears, our sales cease, all the consumers turn to him, and a branch of French industry whose ramifications are innumerable is all at once reduced to complete stagnation. This rival, which is none other than the sun, is waging war on us so mercilessly that we suspect he is being stirred up against us by perfidious Albion [England], particularly because he has for that haughty island a respect that he does not show for us.

We ask you to be so good as to pass a law requiring the closing of all windows, dormers, skylights, inside and outside shutters, curtains, casements, bulls-eyes, deadlights and blinds; in short, all openings, holes, chinks and fissures through which the light of the sun is wont to enter houses; to the detriment of the fair industries with which, we are proud to say, we have endowed the country, a country that cannot, without betraying ingratitude, abandon us today to so unequal a combat.

Be good enough, honorable deputies, to take our request seriously, and do not reject it without at least hearing the reasons that we have to advance in its support. First, if you shut off as much as possible all access to natural light, and therefore create a need for artificial light, what industry in France will not ultimately be encouraged? If France consumes more tallow, there will have to be more cattle and sheep; and consequently we shall see an increase in cleared fields, meat, wool, leather, and especially manure, the basis of all agricultural wealth.

If France consumes more oil, we shall see an expansion in the cultivation of the poppy, the olive and rapeseed. These rich yet soil-exhausting plants will come at just the right time to enable us to put to profitable use the increased fertility that the breeding of cattle will impart to the land. Our moors will be covered with resinous trees. Numerous swarms of bees will gather from our mountains the perfumed treasures that today waste their fragrance, like the flowers from which they emanate. Thus, there is not one branch of agriculture that would not undergo a great expansion.

The same holds true of shipping. Thousands of vessels will engage in whaling, and in a short time we shall have a fleet capable of upholding the honor of France and of gratifying the patriotic aspirations of the undersigned petitioners, chandlers and etc. But what shall we say of the *specialties* of Parisian manufacture? Henceforth you will behold gilding, bronze, and crystal in candlesticks, in lamps, in chandeliers, in candelabra sparkling in spacious emporia compared with which, those of today are but stalls.

There is no needy resin collector on the heights of his sand dunes, no poor miner in the depths of his black pit, who will not receive higher wages and enjoy increased prosperity. It needs but a little reflection, gentlemen, to be convinced that there is perhaps not one Frenchman, from the wealthy stockholder of the Anzin Company to the humblest vendor of matches, whose condition would not be improved by the success of our petition.

It is probably most ironic that after a genteel country existence for most of his life, and at the moment he finally found his place as a leader in economic thought, Bastiat's health failed him; he had contracted tuberculosis. In spite of his weakening health, the pace of events in France and Bastiat's level of commitment and responsibility were both increased. As the revolution of 1848 swept Louis Philippe off the throne and the Second Republic was declared, Bastiat ran for and won election as a deputy to the National Assembly.

Bastiat saw clearly that with the tumultuous happenings in Paris and his health so fragile, he might never live to return to his estate. He was absolutely convinced that he must do whatever he could to stop the socialist tide that seemed to accompany the new revolution. Unfortunately, after the king was deposed, chaos reigned. Accounts of the scenes in Paris depict angry mobs stalking the streets, Parisians starving in their homes, and bedlam in the Assembly.

Though racked by his debilitating disease and frustrated with life in the Assembly, Bastiat churned out a remarkable series of pamphlets and essays addressing a wide variety of economic issues. He at last produced his most famous book, *The Law*. In this slim volume Bastiat captured the most profound truths of the nature of freedom and the proper role of government.

Bastiat declared, "Life, faculties, production; in other words, individuality, liberty, prosperity, this is man. And in spite of the cunning of artful political leaders, these three gifts from God precede all human legislation, and are superior to it. Life, liberty and property do not exist because men have made laws. On the contrary, it was the fact that life, liberty and property existed beforehand that caused men to make laws."

He also identified the natural tendency of government to develop its own powers and to impose its will on the people. Bastiat held that the tendencies of a socialist government amounted to legalized plunder, which he described in this way: "When a portion of wealth is transferred from the person who owns it, without his consent and without compensation, and whether by force or fraud to anyone who does not own it, then I say that property is violated; that an act of plunder has been committed." He emphatically stated that the origin of law was to protect life, liberty, and property. When the law is used to violate those things, then the law has been perverted:

> Socialism, like the ancient ideas from which it springs, confuses the distinction between government and society. As a result of this, every time we object to a thing being done by government, the socialists conclude that we object to its being done at all. We disapprove of state education. Then the socialists say that we are opposed to any education. We object to a state religion. Then the socialists say that we want no religion at all. We object to a state enforced equality. Then they say that we are against equality. And so on, and so on. It is as if the socialists were to accuse us of not wanting persons to eat because we do not want the state to raise grain.

Bastiat painfully and desperately argued for a system in which the government engaged in no plunder: "This is the principle of justice, peace, order, stability, harmony and logic. Until the day of my death I shall proclaim this principle with all the force of my lungs, which is all too inadequate." Within a year of writing these profound words, Frederic Bastiat died. His last words are reported to have been, "The truth, the truth!"

Bastiat is often portrayed as a man standing alone against the turmoil of revolutionary France. In the wake of his passing, France's socialist democracy collapsed, and Louis Napoleon returned the nation to rule by empire.

The measure of greatness is not always possible to determine at the moment it occurs. Indeed, we often see that what appears to be great and wonderful at the time is later revealed to be hopelessly flawed. With Frederic Bastiat, he found inspiration late in his life to help lead a fiery national debate about how fundamental government policies affect the lives of citizens. He struggled against both his deteriorating health and the prevailing political tide, convinced of the rightness of his position and the necessity that he join the battle. He did so eloquently and tirelessly, but despite spending himself in the struggle, his arguments did not carry the day.

In the here and now, his voice continues to ring with the truth about the nature and purpose of a free government. One hundred and fifty years later, his words continue to resonate through history and are the finest measure of his greatness.

CONGRESSMAN
JON CHRISTENSEN

CONGRESS OF THE UNITED STATES
HOUSE OF REPRESENTATIVES

THE SECOND DISTRICT OF NEBRASKA

At age thirty-one, Congressman Christensen was one of the youngest members elected to the GOP freshmen class of the 104th Congress. He grew up in the farming community of Saint Paul, Nebraska. Christensen entered Midland Lutheran College on a full basketball scholarship in 1981, and graduated in 1985, majoring in business and biology. He entered South Texas College of Law and received his law degree in 1989. Following law school, Christensen entered the insurance field as vice president of the corporate division of COMReP, Inc. In 1991 he accepted a position as marketing director for Aquila Group, a holding company for Old MacDonalds, a distributor of an organic fertilizer.

Christensen is a member of the Nebraska Farm Bureau, the Nebraska Cattlemen's Association, the National Federation of Independent Business, the Northwest Rotary Club, and the National and Omaha Associations of Life Underwriters.

Representative Christensen's Second District includes the Omaha region and part of Cass County. He was among the first freshmen Republicans to be named to the House Ways and Means Committee since George Bush in 1966. As an active member of the Republican Task Force on Legal Reform, Christensen led his freshmen colleagues in an effort to expand the House's product liability reforms. Along with senior members, he succeeded in passing amendments to the legal reform package, enacting medical malpractice reforms, and extending "fair share" reforms to all civil lawsuits.

Christensen is the sponsor of H.R. 1972, the Independent Contractor Tax Simplification Act. The bill would provide a three-factor alternative to the infamous twenty-factor test currently used by the Internal Revenue Service.

Congressman Christensen serves on the Ways and Means Committee and the Health and Social Security Subcommittee. He is a member of the Republican Task Force on Legal Reform.

How to Contact

1020 Longworth House Office Building,
Washington, D.C. 20515
Telephone: 202-225-4155
Fax: 202-225-3032

☆ ☆ ☆ ☆ ☆ ☆ ☆ ☆ ☆ ☆ ☆ ☆ ☆

On the northwestern corner of the University of Nebraska Memorial Stadium is this inscription: COURAGE, GENEROS-ITY, FAIRNESS, HONOR; IN THESE ARE THE TRUE AWARDS OF MANLY SPORTS. Many Nebraska fans are fond of pointing to the Nebraska Cornhuskers' head football coach, Tom Osborne, as the living embodiment of those words. If one more value could be added to that list to describe him, it would be persistence or, as Tom might say, stick-to-itiveness.

Coach Osborne is the *winningest active coach* within a decade or more of college football today, and he perseveres not just in his pursuit of excellence but also in his commitment to himself, his family, his great team, and his God. Coach Osborne's lasting dedication to his ideals is a moral beacon not just to his players or Big Red fans, but to every young person in America who trembles in anticipation of a kickoff. In a moral climate where sports figures are easily caught up in webs of greed and self-indulgence, Osborne's perseverance sets him apart.

Tom Osborne has excelled throughout his long sporting career. After making a comeback from what to lesser men would be devastating losses in championship games, he recovered from the losses and persevered, coaching one great season after another. The crown jewels of Osborne's career were the triumphant wins of the national championship in 1995 and 1996. Tom Osborne was able to withstand the withering pressures of Big Eight football for twenty-three years in the same club without ever posting a losing season, then took home the biggest prize of all, the national championship trophy, twice! And he did it all with an iron grip on his humility.

John E. Roberts, then executive vice president of the Fellowship of Christian Athletes, and another man I look up to a great deal, once said of Osborne, "He's also honest, uncompromisingly honest." That uncompromising character and the determination

53

to remain true to himself project his exceptional standing as a role model to the young people he leads. Those traits also persuaded me to write this chapter in the first place! Tom Osborne's persistence is an attribute to which we should all aspire.

Tom Osborne came into the world on February 23, 1937, in Hastings, Nebraska. To no one's surprise, he developed into a fine young athlete, playing three years of football at Hastings High School. As a teenager, his sports achievements led to his selection as Nebraska High School Athlete of the Year. Continuing his winning style, Osborne topped his high school record while at Hastings College by winning State College Athlete of the Year, not once, but twice! He received his bachelor's degree in 1959.

Osborne played three years of professional football, two with the Washington Redskins and one with the San Francisco 49ers. While playing for the 49ers, Osborne's roommate and fellow player was another personal hero of mine, Jack Kemp, the former congressman and secretary of Housing and Urban Development. His revolutionary ideas about taxes and empowerment helped shape the political thinking of an entire generation of Reagan conservatives. After leaving San Francisco, Osborne continued his education, receiving both a master's degree and a Ph.D. in educational psychology from the University of Nebraska.

Osborne's amazing coaching career is a story of determination and excellence, spanning twenty-two tough years in college football before culminating in that most coveted prize, the national championship. Among active coaches with at least a decade of coaching under their belt, those many years of near misses propelled Osborne to the top of the winner's list. His incredible record might at first be mistaken for a misprint, a startling 82 percent win record, ranking him eighth among all football coaches in the history of the game. Under Osborne's leadership, the Huskers won the Big Eight crown in 1975, 1978, 1981 through 1984, 1988, and 1991 through 1995. Every single team Tom Osborne coached landed a slot in a prestigious bowl game, for a grand total bettered only by Paul "Bear" Bryant of Alabama and Joe Paterno of Penn State.

A career of such magnitude was not without some pain. In 1984, Osborne's Huskers fell to Miami University in the Orange Bowl by only one point, 31–30, when Turner Gill's two-point conversion pass, needed to win the game, was tipped away in the end zone by an opposing player. Though I remember admiring the sheer guts it took to make that last play call, the Nebraska fans were plunged into despair over the loss. The incident left Osborne nearly unruffled, and in his autobiography *More Than Winning*, he related his feelings about the experience: "As I reflected after the game, I felt our demeanor, the attitude of the players, and the courage they had shown really were superlative. I was disappointed, and yet it was certainly not a shattering experience."

The action in 1994 was again at the FedEx Orange Bowl, and the Huskers had battled to a one-point lead over Florida State, only to see their lead evaporate by a Florida field goal in the last few moments of the game. Every Nebraska fan shared the heartbreak of seeing that tremendous winning season snapped at the very end by a single, tumbling kick. It was then Coach Osborne displayed his perseverance most clearly.

The next season, 1994–95, must have been haunted by the pain of those final losses, especially the last one to Florida State. Only a perfect performance would net the Huskers the sought-after NCAA championship. With the blindingly fast and powerful Tommie Frazier in the quarterback slot at the beginning of the season, the Huskers seemed to have what it would take to go all the way, but when injury sidelined one superstar, it was up to another young quarterback, Brook Berringer, to carry the season and keep the team on the right track.

In the 1994–95 contests, Nebraska topped the list again for ground yardage gained, the ninth time since 1980; the team chalked up a second straight undefeated season and the fourth straight league title! Time and time again, the Big Red seemed doomed during a game, but they fought back with sheer willpower and pulled out the win. That performance over the regular season landed the team and "Doctor Tom" back in Miami, earning Osborne his third consecutive Big Eight Coach of the Year award.

Of course, that game is history, a triumph for Coach Osborne and every Nebraska fan. The team trailed for most of the game, but the team stamina that is instilled in every Osborne squad increasingly allowed the Huskers to dominate the proceedings both offensively and defensively. With dazzling displays of prowess by the injured Frazier and the rocket-armed Berringer, the Huskers slowly gained the lead and won the Orange Bowl and the national championship, 24–17. Having just been elected to Congress, I was forced to watch the game on TV in Washington, D.C. I made sure that my family and I surrounded ourselves with plenty of roaring Husker fans. It seemed, if we listened closely, we could hear the cheers of Nebraska fans all the way from home! The Huskers had finally cleaned up their "unfinished business"— and were to go on to repeat the accomplishment the next year.

As his autobiography explains, Osborne's football program is directed toward "more than winning." It is aimed at turning out well-rounded, well-educated, and talented young men. In direct contrast to some coaches, Osborne's approach to his team is very positive. Tom describes it this way: "I don't use profanity. I try to avoid being negative and don't use hatred toward opponents as a motivational or coaching tool. Rather, we talk about respecting our opponents, not retaliating, and about controlling the environment of a game by our actions, to make it as positive as we can."

Amidst the dizzying temptations that accompany international renown as a coaching great, Osborne has remained true to his institution—not just for twenty-three consecutive seasons, but for twenty-four memorable years. He has stayed with the school he loves through tough times and lean, while remaining committed to extracting the best his players had to offer rather than getting the best deal he could obtain for himself.

The best those players have to offer applies to the classroom as well as to the field. Osborne allows no slackers when it comes to studying or using football skills as a substitute for the primary reason for being in college. In testament to his commitment to developing the man, and not just the athlete, more than 80 percent of Osborne's players have stepped forward on graduation day to claim their degree. In addition, the University of Nebraska football program tops the list of recipients for nearly every academic honor dedicated to college athletes. Nebraska has twenty-three NCAA postgraduate scholarship winners and fifteen National Football Foundation and Hall of Fame Scholar-Athlete awards.

Still, Osborne goes a step farther. His young men must dedicate themselves to their play, their studies, and their community. Through their community outreach efforts, his players reach more than fifty thousand children a year. Tom and his wonderful wife, Nancy, established the Husker Teammates program that joins the hands of the players and at-risk Lincoln, Nebraska, area junior high students in a special big brother–type relationship. The program receives funding from the Osborne Endowment for Youth, which the coach pioneered with his own money, in a selfless effort to keep kids in school at the secondary level and beyond. With Osborne's determined shepherding, that endowment has grown quickly. The banquet held to honor Osborne's 200th win raised an astonishing $250,000 for his cause.

Tom Osborne has shown a resolute and unswerving commitment to his ideals, his values, and his team. He is a Nebraskan by birth, who stayed a Nebraskan by choice while facing a multitude of temptations and distractions. His persistence on and off the playing field has earned him the respect of the entire nation, and the undying admiration of at least one fan I can name, Jon Christensen.

Coach Osborne's stick-to-itiveness establishes him as a leader of more than a football team. Sports-minded kids in schools across America follow his proactive display of principles and positive attitude. I attended Midland Lutheran College in Nebraska, a school very similar to Osborne's alma mater, Hastings. I played basketball instead of football, and Tom Osborne coached me from a distance, whether he knew it or not.

His steady determination has inspired me. Today I still strive to match his ability to overcome obstacles, the strength with which he holds tight to his faith, and his even-tempered leadership. I have found that setting goals and stretching to achieve them with all my might, as Coach Osborne has done, are among the most rewarding aspects of my life. Osborne's single-minded determination and faith are models to me of the right way to live. Coach Osborne was a beacon in my life, showing me that commitment to God and commitment to achieving greatness in a sport were linked. Osborne helped me understand that faith is the reason for achievement; that playing only for yourself is ultimately empty, and playing for something greater than yourself is ultimately fulfilling.

Osborne warns us that the hardest thing about coaching "is the temptation to put other things before my faith. One of the biggest temptations is to make winning or being successful 'in the world's eyes' more important than anything else." These words, and others like them from Coach Osborne, ring absolutely true to me. When I put aside myself and the worry of how other people may view me, I feel the best about what I do.

Coach Osborne is an active member of the Fellowship of Christian Athletes (FCA). In *More Than Winning*, he related this personal experience about his first FCA meeting, "The impact was deep and led to a personal commitment, a time when my faith really became my own and not a second-hand faith that somebody else wanted me to have." Like Osborne, I have felt a sustained effect on my life because of FCA. I was the proud cofounder of Midland Lutheran's FCA, which grew to one hundred members by the time I graduated. Holding up Coach Osborne's dedication to his beliefs helped lead me to my most rewarding experiences.

In terms of sheer drive, Osborne tells a story about the only athletic pursuit he ever disliked, running the 440-yard dash in track. Yet, he did it almost compulsively until he had worked his time down to a scant forty-nine seconds! It's this kind of stick-to-itiveness I've always tried to achieve in basketball, in track, and in life. When I was a high school sophomore, a friend bet me I couldn't run two miles. Well, I did it, but I wasn't sure he was wrong because it hurt so much! I went on to set five high school track records, and I'm glad my friend made that bet.

Similarly, when I was a member of the basketball squad at Saint Paul's High School in my hometown, I visualized the goal of being the best basketball player in Nebraska. I don't know whether I actually reached that goal or not, but in my senior year I was thrilled to be voted the most valuable player in the Nebraska High School Coaches All-Star Game. Witnessing the living, breathing example of persistence by Tom Osborne made a difference in my life, as I'm sure it has in the lives of many others.

The world needs more Tom Osbornes. I believe that the value of character attributes such as persistence has been weakened in American society. For many, thoughts of holding fast to goals, ideals, and religious faith have been swept aside by morals of convenience and a lifestyle focused on self-indulgence. Confronted by academic failure in school, students give up on education and drop out. Constantly bombarded with the alleged rewards of a permissive culture, college students forsake the family values and hometown virtues in which they were raised and dabble in drugs and promiscuity. Some never recover from the experimentation. Faced with the overwhelming onslaught of a nearly valueless media and entertainment industry, parents surrender their most sacred beliefs to a secular world and allow their children to grow up without a proactive faith. That is why I say the world needs more Coach Osbornes.

Perhaps more obvious, though less fundamental, is the dual disaster of losing perseverance toward family and work. These necessary underpinnings of a strong society have been steadily snipped away from all directions. Most of us have heard the frightening statistic that one American baby in every three is born to an unwed mother. The child is also born to a father devoid of the perseverance to uphold the awesome responsibility the title implies. America's explosive divorce rate is the quick and easy way out of an unpleasant situation, but breaks the cord that binds families together.

Large segments of our population who once worked to support themselves have dropped off the charts into permanent unemployment. They have no trade, no job, and no future. Coach Osborne diligently tries to instill a work ethic in his players that pays off during a game and during preparation for the next game. Too many kids go without this influence, and the only message they receive is that they can skateboard through life, happily channel surfing and accepting handouts from enabling government programs.

Perhaps what bothers me the most in American society is that our government ranks prominently among the reasons that qualities such as perseverance are gradually slipping away from us. Public education, clogged by sluggish bureaucracies and outright incompetence, loses sight of its basic mission and weakens our national commitment to learning. The liberal outposts of the courts and their allies in the American Civil Liberties Union work to stamp out any warm cinder of religion from our public squares.

Aid to Families with Dependent Children (AFDC) writes checks to single parents living away from their partners, and often increases the stipend if another unwed birth occurs. This is probably the most emotionally and economically weak family structure it is possible to support.

At the same time, Supplemental Security Income (SSI) writes checks to drug addicts and alcoholics to help them recover from their addiction *without a single documented recovery in the entire history of the program!* Looming over these issues, Congress itself has refused to muster the perseverance and strength to balance the federal budget. When I ran for office, I had never before held a government position. I saw taxes punishing those who work to pay for the very programs that crush the values I hold dear. I witnessed our leaders in Washington arrogantly dismiss what I believe in, and then spend Nebraska citizens' money to overregulate Nebraska. The government assault on persistence, on faith, and on the American family dragged me into politics.

I was brought to Washington in the great watershed election of 1994, and in my perspective, the people were voting to restore values to our government. I know that in all I do here, I will try to hold up Tom Osborne as the ideal model of persistence, hard work, and faith. If I could throw out all the politics, all the policy, and even all the effects his persistence had on me, I still know this truth: America needs more Tom Osbornes.

CONGRESSWOMAN
BARBARA CUBIN

CONGRESS OF THE UNITED STATES
HOUSE OF REPRESENTATIVES

FOR ALL WYOMING

Representative Cubin is a fifth-generation Wyomingite with roots in Casper. She is married to Dr. Frederick W. Cubin, and they have two sons, William and Frederick III. Cubin graduated from Natrona High School and earned a degree in chemistry from Creighton University in 1969.

From 1975 to 1994, Representative Cubin managed the business office for Dr. Cubin. She has also worked as a teacher and a social worker for the state of Wyoming, conducted minority and veterans training for the Department of Labor, and worked as a chemist for the Wyoming Machinery Company.

Cubin's political and civic involvement is extensive. She served in the Wyoming state senate, and also in the Wyoming state house of representatives from 1987 to 1992. She has been a member of the National Council of State Legislatures and the Executive Committee of the Energy Council. She was awarded a Toll Fellowship by the Council for State Government for her leadership ability. In 1994, Cubin was named Edison Electric

Institute's Wyoming Legislator of the Year for energy and environmental issues.

Among her Republican activities, Cubin has been chairwoman of the Wyoming Senate Conference, precinct committeewoman, legislative liaison, and state convention parliamentarian. She is an active participant in many civic groups in Casper and is an officer and board member for several organizations.

Cubin is vice-chair of the Committee on Resources and a member of the Science Committee. She also serves on four subcommittees.

How to Contact

> 1114 Longworth House Office Building,
> Washington, D.C. 20515
> Telephone: 202-225-2311
> Fax: 202-225-3057

☆ ☆ ☆ ☆ ☆ ☆ ☆ ☆ ☆ ☆ ☆ ☆ ☆

The selfless examples of many well-known historic and modern figures have helped me and others set goals and expectations of our own. Among them was Abraham Lincoln, sixteenth president of the United States. In his farewell address to his fellow citizens in Springfield, Illinois, President Lincoln expressed his reluctance to leave his home and relocate to Washington, D.C. He lamented,

> No one not in my situation can appreciate my feeling of sadness at this parting. To this place and to the kindness of this people, I owe everything. Here I have lived a quarter of a century and have passed from a young man to an old man. Here my children have been born and one is buried. I now leave, not knowing when or whether ever I may return, with a task before me greater than that which rested upon [George] Washington. Without the assistance of that Divine Being who ever attended him, I cannot succeed. With that assistance, I cannot fail. Trusting in Him, who can go with me and remain with you, and be everywhere for good, let us confidently hope that all yet will be well.

Leaving my home in Wyoming to live in Washington, D.C., took more courage and caused more sadness than I thought were in me, but Lincoln's example was a good one. His compassion for others, his commitment to principles, and especially his personal courage created a stirring inside and an uneasiness that pushed me beyond a comfort level I could easily settle into.

Former British Prime Minister Margaret Thatcher also had an impact on my adult development. I earned a bachelor of science degree in chemistry from Creighton University and worked as a chemist early in my career. Margaret Thatcher was also a chemist by training. These comments from Mrs. Thatcher show how the logic and straightforward thinking required in the field of chemistry affected her later involvement in politics: "I think that it should interest you in the problems of finding out as much as you can about the way we work, the way matter is put together, and it should give you an interest in using the results." The stable thinking of her chemistry background also gave her the confidence and courage to candidly comment about the issues, even to President Ronald Reagan, by announcing, "I'm a chemist; I KNOW it won't work!"

From one of my favorite interviews in the *Washington Post*, Mrs. Thatcher said, "Look at a day when you are supremely satisfied, just at the end of the day. It's not a day when you lounge around doing nothing. It's when you've had everything to do, a real challenge, and you've done it! Life really isn't just an existence, it's using all the talents with which you were born." Lady Thatcher's example has helped me immensely to grow in confidence and courage.

Two world leaders I admired for their courage since my high school days are Anwar Sadat of Egypt and Menachem Begin of Israel. They were highly regarded as two of this century's great statesmen as they undertook one of the major peace initiatives of all time, when Sadat went to Israel in 1977 for the conference that led to the 1979 Egyptian-Israeli peace treaty. For that monumental work they shared the 1978 Nobel Peace Prize. Anwar Sadat was assassinated by Muslim extremists while reviewing a military parade in 1981. This quote from a speech just prior to his death clearly portrays his compassion and courage:

> Any life that is lost in war is a human life, be it that of an Arab or an Israeli. Innocent children who are deprived of the care and compassion of their parents are ours, they are ours if they are living on Arab or Israeli land. For the sake of them, for the sake of the lives of our sons and brothers, for the sake of affording our communities the opportunity to work for the progress and happiness of man, feeling secure and with the right to a dignified life, for the generations to

come, for a smile on the face of every child born in our land. For all that, I have made my decision to come to you, despite the hazards, to deliver my address.

From my earliest memories I have sensed an obligation to care for others, serve with commitment, share with anyone in need, and hold fast to the knowledge that there are an absolute right and an absolute wrong. Where have such convictions come from in my life? From the most influential people in my life—my parents. Time after time they amazed me with their demonstrations of charity, courage, loyalty, and commitment. I learned more lessons by watching what my parents actually did than by hearing what they told me to do. Because they are human, they are not perfect people, and they were not perfect parents. But I sincerely believe what they taught me through their words and deeds were the virtues I needed to live a productive, healthy, and full life.

So that others might understand the strength of conviction of the individuals in my family, I offer a few historical excerpts. My maternal great-grandfather moved to Wyoming, probably from Missouri, about 1847. In those days, Wyoming was not even a territory; it was the wild frontier! It was also the era of the mountain man, who made his entire living from the land and its bounty. That is exactly how my great-grandfather lived. He was a trapper, and he traded furs with Native Americans.

On my father's side of the family, my grandmother homesteaded in Wyoming with her sister, and they did so as single women, claiming adjoining tracts. Their family came from Nebraska, and it is reported their father built the very first prefabricated housing. He assembled the walls and roof joists for both cabins, hauled them on a truck to the Casper area, and put them together right on the homestead site. When the job was complete, he returned to his farm in Nebraska. Both my parents came from hardy pioneer stock.

Both my parents were previously married, and Mother supported her four children from that prior union with no assistance from anyone. She worked at three jobs to do it and traded baby-sitting services with a friend to work out the schedule. Father had three children from his first marriage. In their mid-twenties, my parents married and combined their two families. That meant there were seven kids in the house, ranging in age from two to eight years. Mother was employed outside the house intermittently, but I remember her most often at home, devoting her time to seven children and tending to a twenty-room house.

We children were adopted by the parent we had not been born to, thus eliminating many thoughtless questions such as, "Who are hers, and who are his?" Mother earned the largest credit for raising the children since Father traveled five days a week to support us. Because he traveled so much, the memories of his contributions to our lessons in life are not as numerous as those from my mother. They are, however, just as deeply ingrained. My father is the most honest person I have ever known, not only in words, but also in his actions. He told us, "Never do in private what you wouldn't do in the presence of someone else." He was a hard-working, dependable, and sincere man. He was also a strict disciplinarian. Though he loved his family and provided well for us, he found it difficult to communicate that love. I believe he has made up for that through the love he has shown to his grandchildren.

I remember the time when my biological father came to Casper, Wyoming, where we lived. It was his misfortune to be beaten and robbed. An emergency room worker at the hospital called our house because that was the only phone number he was able to provide. My father answered the phone and was told my biological father was there and needed help. Father went to the hospital, paid the bill, and took him to a motel. Father then left money at the desk for two weeks' rent of the room and any food he might eat in the restaurant. On the way out, he told the desk clerk, "Call me if he needs anything else." I know of few people who would so generously and honestly care for another in that way, especially under unusual family circumstances. I must say that there was never a moment in my life that I didn't absolutely know that my father loved and respected me.

My father taught me that a good reputation was your most valuable possession. He taught me to be reliable; he insisted I could achieve anything I really wanted to achieve. He encouraged me to set aside the fear that comes with attempting higher achievements. His own courage in choosing, at age twenty-four, to be responsible for seven children, combined with his diligence, resulted in his becoming a very successful businessman. I don't know anyone who doesn't love and respect my father, especially me.

When I think about all the people who have touched my life in some way, my mother has been the most loving and influential one. Observing her courage and determination in overcoming the emotional trauma at the death of my older brother, Gary, in 1969 was an inspiration to me and many others. Mother faced many hardships in her life, but she was always larger than her troubles and overcame them.

Her courage, charity, and true friendship are but a few of the virtues she introduced into others' lives. The following are a few of the excerpts from a book compiled by her family and friends and presented to my mother on her sixtieth birthday. They reveal who she really is. They portray a noble, courageous, strong, generous, and kind person.

In part, her son wrote, "A lady in every sense of the word; very kind, extremely honest and trustworthy."

From her grandson: "When I come for advice you always give me good ideas, even if they're not what I want to hear."

From Mother's niece: "I also can call you FRIEND!"

From her nephew: "And who was the dear, dear person that caused me to be reminded that the really important things in life included honor, compassion, humor, caring, family and respect? It was you, of course."

From a woman I call my sister because our whole family "adopted" her more than twenty years ago, when she had no family to call her own: "Not many people have been afforded the luxury that I had when it came to choosing my mother. I was able to make this choice over a number of years, while [watching you] and evaluating the qualities I envied and felt most essential in life."

And finally, this is a part of what I wrote to Mother on her sixtieth birthday: *"You're just like your mother!* I stand tall and proud anytime I hear it, even today. Any good you see in me is a reflection of yourself. I've always been proud to share your name. Our friendship is my most valuable possession. You are the most magnificent woman I have ever known. I love you, Mother."

When I was a little girl, I wanted to be either a doctor or president of the United States! I watched my cousin's German shepherd have puppies in a window well, and I did my part in assisting with the delivery by pushing my way to the front so I could see the actual birth. Right then and there, the miracle of a new life and the immediate love I felt for those puppies told me I wanted to become a doctor. Or so I thought at the time.

I still love to see new life come into the world, and I have been fortunate to watch the birth of two of my niece's babies. The miracle of life is still breathtaking to me. My husband is a physician, and perhaps the goal of becoming a doctor that I had as a young girl has been vicariously fulfilled through him. As for being president, we'll have to wait and see.

It is with humility that I thank God for His Son, the famous people, and the not quite so famous who have helped me become who I am today. It is with deep faith that I accept the challenges placed before me in the 104th Congress, and I remain steadfast in fulfilling my promise to help turn this great United States of America back to the people.

CONGRESSMAN
THOMAS M. DAVIS III

CONGRESS OF THE UNITED STATES
HOUSE OF REPRESENTATIVES

THE ELEVENTH DISTRICT OF VIRGINIA

Congressman Davis, a native of Minot, North Dakota, moved to Virginia as a young man and graduated from Amherst College with a B.A. in 1971 and from the University of Virginia with a J.D. in 1975. He lives in Falls Church with his wife, the former Margaret "Peggy" Rantz, and their three children. An avid baseball fan, Davis has been active in attempts to attract a major league baseball team to northern Virginia. He has worked as a lawyer, a professional services firm executive, and a legislative aide.

Davis's political career began in 1979 with his election to the Fairfax County Board of Supervisors. In 1991, Davis challenged the incumbent Democratic chairman of the board and won by an astonishing two to one ratio.

In 1994, Davis was elected to the Eleventh District congressional seat with 53 percent of the vote. Created in 1990 as a result of redistricting, the Eleventh District includes the northern Virginia–Washington, D. C., suburbs and parts of Fairfax and Prince William Counties.

Davis serves on the Government Reform and Oversight Committee and the Science Committee. He is a member of five subcommittees.

How to Contact

> 415 Cannon House Office Building,
> Washington, D.C. 20515
> Telephone: 202-225-1492
> Fax: 202-225-3071

☆ ☆ ☆ ☆ ☆ ☆ ☆ ☆ ☆ ☆ ☆ ☆ ☆

I am most grateful for this opportunity to pay tribute to the very special person who has exerted the strongest influence on my life and still remains my most positive role model. Anyone who even slightly knows me will attest that the person who continues to inspire me more than any other is my mother, Dorothy Van Patten Davis.

Mom was born in the agricultural community of Hastings, Nebraska, in 1917. Her people were hardworking, family oriented, and solidly middle class. They lived according to the simple rules their forebears had set down for them. They believed you had to make your own way in the world. The rewards of hard work, both personal and material, were instilled in their children along with lessons in self-reliance gained from their own experiences.

They were the kind of people that fifty years later, during the Nixon era, the media would describe as middle Americans. They believed you worked hard and saved what you could. You did your duty for your family, your neighbors, and your community, and you expected no thanks or praise. In other words, they did what was expected of them, and they looked to their children to do the same. In their world, you were given no special credit just for showing up, but you could also receive a good thrashing, verbal or otherwise, if you didn't!

Graduating from this environment, Mother left Lincoln High School and went off to college. She majored in psychology at the University of Nebraska and earned a master's degree in that field. Mother began to make her way in one of the two professions open to women in the pre–World War II era. She became a teacher. (The alternative would have been nursing.) She showered her students with the loving care, attention, and drive to succeed that each of her own five children later came to recognize and appreciate.

Through her work, vivacious personality, and exceptional

good looks (which I did not inherit), she caught the eye of another young teacher, whose name I carry. They were married in 1948. Their jobs and a yearning to plant roots of their own took them to North Dakota where I was born. Not long after, they moved our young family to northern Virginia for what I thought then, and continue to feel now, was an extraordinary reason. My paternal grandfather, Clarence Alva Davis, had accepted a prominent post in President Eisenhower's administration.

Grandfather's family was expected to be on hand to support him and to help him make history. A more fair way to put it would be that his wife, son, and daughter-in-law were to watch him. He had a knack for letting his grandchildren believe they were "helping." Worthy of a praiseful essay in his own right, Grandfather Clarence was already a legend in Nebraska by the time Ike beckoned him to Washington, D.C. Brilliantly fresh out of Harvard Law School, he became, at age twenty-five, the youngest attorney general in the history of our state. He was a conscientious man, dedicated to his conservative political principles, and he took his duties as a public servant very seriously.

One trait he possessed was that he was not extremely deferential to his elders when he thought they were wrong. A United States senator who quickly found that out was George Norris. Grandfather came from Grand Beaver County, Norris from Cooke County. Norris was a feisty Progressive committed to an ever enlarging federal government. Grandfather was an aggressive conservative dedicated to the restraints on government he saw spelled out in the Constitution. Although it was inevitable they would clash, the two prairie politicians were always searching for more colorful and flamboyant ways to emphasize their opposing positions. Their antics provided constituents with much comic relief during the dreary days of the Great Depression.

Observing my grandfather rubbing elbows with the great leaders of the day opened entire new worlds to me and stirred my imagination as I was growing up in the Washington, D.C., area. My siblings and I came to anticipate the events with increasing eagerness, and as diversions, because of the storm that had erupted at home. My father's continuing battle with alcoholism eventually consumed him. He squandered his money, lost several jobs, and stood a two-year tour in the Virginia state prison system. Before I reached adulthood, he and my mother had divorced and remarried several times.

Throughout that agonizing period, Mother displayed the stamina, courage, and perseverance that have so framed her character in the hearts of her children. With the fastidiousness of Harry Truman (I use Truman because he was a president Mom didn't always agree with, but greatly respected), she made several tough decisions and stuck to them.

She resolved, first, that the family would stay together, second, that she would become the primary breadwinner, and third, that her kids would do more than just survive the experiences that lay ahead for all of us. She insisted that we excel in all we undertook. Mom drew inspiration from her faith that gave her confidence our family's needs would be met. For all this to happen, Dorothy Van Patten Davis knew that nothing short of the complete mobilization of the entire family would suffice. She molded five growing children into a highly effective "fighting unit," appointing herself as commander. A strong dose of Nebraska stick-to-itiveness had taken hold on the banks of the Potomac.

Immediately, Mother returned to work. She cared for other people's children at our home during the day so she could be there with us. She waited on tables at night, after my older sister arrived home from school to care for us. On weekends Mom continued to mind other people's children and worked odd jobs at home. My brothers and I found paper routes and mowed lawns while my sister began a baby-sitting career. All the money we earned was deposited into a common pool and spent, or saved for some purpose, in accordance with the budget my mother diligently devised.

Equal in importance to the life-changing decisions she made and discipline she displayed and imposed was what she gave to us of herself. Mom went to great lengths to help my brother, who had been born blind. Much of our family's daily routine was organized around her decree that he never be made to feel left out of a family activity or different from other people. With me, she noticed I was not reading on the same grade level as other children she was instructing in religious studies, so she withdrew me from public school and sent me to a private one, even though money was tight. I was not allowed to attend public school again until I was reading above my normal grade level.

My mother actively encouraged the fledgling interest I was developing in politics, and she suggested I apply to be a congressional page. I landed the job, and much to my delight, I wound up working for U.S. Senators Carl Curtis and Roman Hruska, both from Nebraska. (What other delegation would I have considered?) Since I couldn't drive, guess whose job it became to drive me to and from the Capitol, with uncertain hours from early morning to late at night? As if she hadn't already enough to do, Mom happily volunteered to provide my transportation. In education, her desire was for me to attend one of the finest colleges, and she urged me to compete for the scholarship I eventually won to Amherst College.

Mom showed equal interest in the hopes and dreams of my brothers and sister. I was fortunate to develop an early interest in politics and major in government while watching my two brothers turn out to be real success stories. One is an engineering graduate of Stanford University; the other is a businessman in Chicago. My sister, not to be one-upped, has the toughest job of all. She is a widowed mother with three children. She has been well prepared for this demanding dual role, learning valuable parenting skills from a master teacher, our mom.

I have often wondered how my mother achieved all these things in only one lifetime. I attribute her indefatigable spirit to her belief in the American dream, her deep faith in God, her sense of humor and, of course, her Nebraska roots. The image of her I will carry in my mind is that of someone always working, always moving, always striving, always looking for and finding the bright spot in any situation.

Today, my mother is retired and living in California, a few blocks from my younger brother. Through my major campaigns in local government and for the House, she worked side by side with me, helping me to achieve my boyhood dream to return to Congress not as a page but as a contributing member. My mother's personal values and the love and commitment to her family that she has never ceased demonstrating will be forever a part of me.

They are the precious gifts of parenthood that I strive every day to pass along to my children. It is my sincere hope that every American mom and dad would do the same.

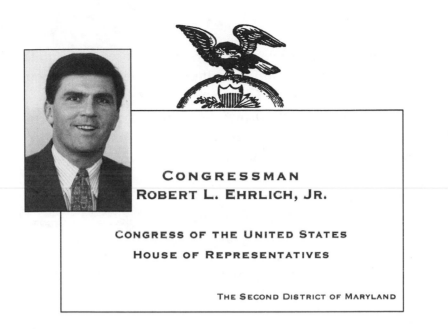

**CONGRESSMAN
ROBERT L. EHRLICH, JR.**

CONGRESS OF THE UNITED STATES
HOUSE OF REPRESENTATIVES

THE SECOND DISTRICT OF MARYLAND

A lawyer by profession, this Baltimore native entered national politics in the 1994 elections. He received 64 percent of the vote, a decisive victory over the Democratic challenger. This first-term victory was especially notable because the second District has a two to one Democratic voter registration advantage.

Ehrlich is a graduate of Princeton University and Wake Forest University School of Law. Athletic and academic scholarships aided him during college and law school. Ehrlich and his wife, Kendel, reside in Timonium.

Although new to the national political scene, Representative Ehrlich has considerable legislative experience. He served in the Maryland House of Delegates from 1987 to 1994. Ehrlich has described himself as a small business advocate and a military hawk. His Congressional priorities include regulatory reform and federal housing policy.

Ehrlich was named Legislator of the Year by the Maryland State Fraternal Order of Police in 1994. He supports the death penalty and tougher sentencing laws. He opposes term limits, and he conservatively cautions colleagues to learn more about how Congress functions before rushing into quick changes.

Congressman Ehrlich is a member of the Government Reform and Oversight Committee and the Banking and Financial Services Committee. He also serves on five subcommittees.

How to Contact
>315 Cannon Office Building,
>Washington, D.C. 20515
>Telephone: 202-225-3061
>Fax: 202-225-3094

☆ ☆ ☆ ☆ ☆ ☆ ☆ ☆ ☆ ☆ ☆ ☆ ☆

From the earliest days of my youth I have been intrigued by that ubiquitously human characteristic we call leadership. Why does one person rise above his peers? What in the human psyche bonds people to their leaders, even to those with whom they sometimes disagree?

When I played football in elementary school, the organized chaos provided my first example of leadership at work and helped me recognize the qualities that make one successful at motivating others. I learned a true leader must have a long-term vision and defined goals. A leader can defend those goals by pitting credibility against criticism while simultaneously exuding confidence his goals can, and will, be met.

I have found that throughout history many people have distinguished themselves as leaders of people and nations. They were waiting in the wings of their destiny until circumstances propelled them, often reluctantly, into a commanding role. Of all the great political leaders who have walked across the world's stage to accept the leader's mantle, few have so impressed and inspired me as Winston S. Churchill.

Churchill led what was, by any standard of achievement, a remarkable life. A poor student in his childhood, who stuttered and spoke with a lisp, he overcame the early hindrances to become a brilliant orator and writer. He was a visionary with an uncanny ability to see the long-term consequences of seemingly insignificant events. He was a skilled politician, yet for much of his public life was politically incorrect and often at odds with fellow members of Parliament and government ministers. At an age when most men would contemplate retirement, the hardy and robust patriot guided his nation through its darkest days in World War II. By the end of his life he enjoyed a worldwide reputation as a scrupulously principled and tough-minded statesman.

Many today regard Winston Churchill as the preeminent political figure of this century. His devotion to the principles of liberty, his intolerance for totalitarianism, and his willingness to fight vigorously, determinedly, and relentlessly for what he believed provided a universal lesson for those of us who aspire to meaningful leadership.

On November 30, 1874, Winston Leonard Spencer Churchill came into the world. He was the eldest son of Lord Randolph Churchill and Lady Churchill (the former Jennie Jerome, an American). From the outset, he was clearly possessed of a strong will and innate stubbornness, and family members and schoolteachers labeled him a disciplinary problem. At the prestigious secondary school Harrow, he was the lowest-ranked student in the class. His father decided that a military career was most appropriate, no doubt hoping the imposed disciplines would set the young Winston on a straighter path. At the age of eighteen Churchill entered that historic learning center for England's elite, the Royal Military College at Sandhurst.

Although he twice failed the entrance exam, he was ultimately accepted. To everyone's relief, Winston warmed quickly to the curriculum and graduated eighth in his class of one hundred fifty. He immediately accepted appointment as a second lieutenant in the 4th Hussars, a cavalry regiment with a long and proud history. Churchill longed for excitement, adventure, and challenge, and he traveled far from England to find all of that. In one episode, Churchill traveled to Cuba while on leave from the army, reporting for a London newspaper on the violent civil war with Spain. Later in life, Churchill is often pictured holding his favorite style of Havana cigar, a taste he acquired while on that mission.

In 1897, while based in Bangalore in southern India, he journeyed to the northwest corner of the English colony again as a reporter, where the fierce Pushtun warriors were battling British troops. He participated in bloody fighting and wrote about the experience in his first book, *The Story of the Malakand Field Force*. A year later, during the British invasion of the Sudan, Churchill took part in his country's last large-scale cavalry charge at the battle of Omdurman. The advent of rapid-fire machine guns and accurate artillery had doomed the military tactic of the cavalry charge.

Winston Churchill was always opinionated and outspoken. He was exceptionally devoted to the British Empire and held his government to the highest of standards. In his second book, *The River War*, which dealt with the Sudanese campaign, Churchill criticized British policy and some of those charged with implementing it, in what would become his trademark manner. His observations were not well received and drew a personal rebuke from the Prince of Wales, the future king of England.

Churchill was possessed with both a sense of personal invulnerability and a belief in his own destiny. After resigning from the army in 1899, Winston began his political career by running an unsuccessful campaign as a Conservative for a parliamentary seat from Oldham. That same year, distant war drums beckoned, and Churchill answered their call. Shortly after arriving in South Africa to report on the Boer War for a London paper, he was captured and imprisoned by the Boers. Never one to sit on his hands, Churchill executed a daring and dramatic escape by scaling a prison wall and stealing rides on freight trains until he had safely emerged from three hundred miles behind the Boer lines, bringing fame and public adulation at home. Upon his return to England, he ran for Parliament again, and the voters of Oldham, despite their Liberal Party loyalties, elected him.

Though a Conservative at heart, Churchill did not mind sharing his views with members of the Liberal opposition. Consequently, he was in disfavor with members of his own party and sharply critical of their policies. Assailed by his Conservative peers, in 1904, he left his old friends behind. Two years later, he ran again and won his old seat in Parliament as a member of the Liberal Party. Beginning in 1906, Churchill held several cabinet positions. In 1911, Prime Minister Herbert Asquith appointed him first lord of the Admiralty. With that authority he determined to maintain British naval superiority over Germany, with whom he was certain war was inevitable. When World War I broke out in 1914, his navy was prepared with a modern and well-equipped fleet.

The following year, Churchill's political career seemed to have ended when he urged an attack on the Turks, a German ally, at Gallipoli Peninsula. The campaign incurred many casualties and was a disastrous defeat for the British. Churchill resigned from the Admiralty but served his country in another position when Prime Minister David Lloyd George appointed him minister of munitions. When World War I ended, he became secretary of state for war, followed quickly by appointment to colonial secretary in 1921.

While recovering from an appendectomy a year later, Churchill lost his reelection bid. Two years later he rejoined the Conservative Party and won back his parliamentary seat. The cycle of Churchill's political star, first rising and then falling, was to repeat itself during his entire career. The 1930s found an old enemy in a state of violent unrest, and Churchill was again warning his countrymen to beware of Germany. In a speech from the floor of the House of Commons in 1932, he warned that Germany must not be allowed to rearm. With typical Churchillian foresight, he predicted that if it was allowed to do so, Germany would soon demand the return of territories lost in World War I. His warnings were mostly ignored, and his emphatic speech did little more than expose him to charges of being a fool and a warmonger. Churchill's experiences during the early and mid-1930s remind one of the biblical admonition: "A prophet is not without honor except in his own country and in his own house" (Matt. 13:57).

Winston Churchill understood that a strong military deters war. He continued to exhort his government to distrust Hitler and to be alert to his intentions, but England was in no mood for a conflict. When Prime Minister Neville Chamberlain agreed at Munich to cede Czechoslovakia to the Third Reich, Churchill was outraged at a policy of appeasement he believed cowardly and immoral. He boldly took to the floor of the House to denounce the agreement and caution the satiation of Hitler would prove to be "the beginning of the reckoning."

Churchill was reappointed to his former post of first lord of the Admiralty when World War II began in September 1939. For England, they were times not only of grave national crisis, but of divisiveness in government over how the war should be conducted. When the government dissolved in 1940 (an ever present possibility under English law), King George VI directed Churchill to form a new government. At sixty-six years of age, Winston Churchill found himself leading his nation into a desperate struggle with a powerful enemy, the outcome of which would determine England's survival as a free democracy. He later wrote that he felt "as if I were walking with destiny, and that all my past life had been but a preparation for this hour and this trial."

In a calm and uplifting manner unequaled in modern history, Churchill rallied his nation to the task at hand. He was realistic and confident, grim yet optimistic. Above all, he was ever mindful of the uncompromising mission that lay ahead, to save England from falling under the boot of Nazi Germany. Only a month after he took office, the British army was evacuated from the beaches at Dunkirk, and the total collapse of France was imminent. England stood alone across the narrow English Channel, awaiting what seemed a near certain German invasion.

In an address to the House of Commons, Churchill thundered

with defiance and resolve, "We shall not flag or fail. We shall go on to the end, we shall fight in France, we shall fight on the seas and oceans, we shall fight with growing confidence and growing strength in the air, we shall defend our island, whatever the cost may be. We shall fight on the beaches, we shall fight on the landing grounds, we shall fight in the fields and in the streets, we shall fight in the hills; we shall never surrender." It was a short speech, long on inspiration, which buoyed the spirit of free people around the world.

Throughout the years of World War II, Churchill led and motivated his nation and much of the free world. He never believed in anything less than total victory over Hitler and his Axis allies. He energized the English people with that goal, even when it seemed impossible. During the course of the war, Churchill epitomized leadership, becoming a virtual icon of steadfastness and resolution. Churchill was England, and England was Churchill.

In the waning days of World War II, with Allied victory certain, the Conservatives were voted out of power, and Churchill became the leader of the loyal opposition. He warned world leaders about the Iron Curtain of communism that was descending across eastern Europe, dimming the light of freedom for all those who remained behind it. Churchill again became prime minister in 1951, finally retiring from public life in April 1955.

I believe an important measure of a leader's ability is his perspective about himself and his role in the affairs of the world. At his eightieth birthday celebration in 1954, Churchill was praised lavishly for his wisdom and guidance during the war. "It was the nation that had the lion's heart," he demurred. "I had the luck to be called on to give the roar."

We live in an extremely interesting but profoundly challenging period in our nation's history. The American people are looking for leadership, but they are not receiving it from our current administration. As a society, our constituents are deciding the direction that we shall go. As a majority in Congress, for the first time in forty years, we Republicans can return our country to responsible fiscal and social policies. We are most fortunate in the House to have Speaker Gingrich and Majority Leader Armey, both of whom possess the optimistic vision and leadership skills that will guide us along our way to building a greater and stronger America.

Like Churchill, these two great Republican leaders are not afraid to stand firm in the courage of their convictions and successfully lead the Congress in our new fiscal and philosophical revolution. These leaders will not surrender, and by working with them, we will not fail.

CONGRESSMAN
MICHAEL P. FORBES

CONGRESS OF THE UNITED STATES
HOUSE OF REPRESENTATIVES

THE FIRST DISTRICT OF NEW YORK

An eastern Long Island native, Congressman Forbes lives in Quogue, Long Island, with his wife, Barbara, and their two children, Abigail and Theodore. The historic congressional seat Forbes holds was first held by Mastic Beach's own William Floyd, a signer of the Declaration of Independence.

Born in Riverhead in 1952, Forbes grew up in Westhampton Beach. He graduated from the State University of New York with a bachelor of arts in history and political science. He began his vocational career by working on the family-owned newspapers, *The News Review* and *The Sunday Review*, founded by his grandfather T. Harold Forbes.

From 1980 to 1983, Forbes was an aide to Representative Alphonse D'Amato. He also served on Congressman Stratton's staff and was chief of staff to Congressman Connie Mack from 1984 to 1987. From 1989 to 1993, Forbes became well known for championing small business while serving under President Bush at the Small Business Administration. He was the architect of an innovative SBA program that created a more customer-oriented environment and increased small business loan volume on Long Island by 300 percent. He also headed his own public relations and marketing firm in the late 1980s. Forbes was regional director and liaison with the House of Representatives for the Chamber of Commerce of the United States.

Representative Forbes is a member of the influential House Appropriations Committee and serves on numerous subcommittees.

How to Contact

502 Cannon House Office Building,
Washington, D.C. 20515
Telephone: 202-225-3826
Fax: 202-225-3143

☆ ☆ ☆ ☆ ☆ ☆ ☆ ☆ ☆ ☆ ☆ ☆ ☆ ☆

As a boy, I was drawn into my mother's weekly ritual of sitting in the sunroom to listen to the unusual Sunday morning broadcasts of Otis G. Pike, our congressman from eastern Long Island.

With impish humor and sardonic wit, Pike would relate the goings-on in Washington, always weaving a colorful anecdote into the weightiness of some pending action in the Congress. Never stilted, boring, or lacking a poke at the crazy doings of the bureaucracy, Pike's weekly musings always managed to turn the seriousness and complexities of Washington politics into something digestible for the folks back home. He made government understandable and interesting while nurturing the seeds of a political career in my thirteen-year-old mind.

Otis Pike is a common man with an uncommon touch. In Washington, D.C., a city not known for its humility, Pike stood out. He could cut through bluster and buffoonery with an uncanny wit that pointedly illuminated the issues.

Otis was born in Riverhead, Long Island, New York, on August 31, 1921, to Otis G. Pike and Belle Lupton. His father worked at the local bank, but died when Otis was only a toddler. Not long after that, Otis also lost his mother. Raised by an aunt, Otis grew up in the same Victorian-style family home where he lives today with his wife, Doris. He attended local schools and was president of his senior class at Riverhead High School. Otis attended Princeton University, from which he graduated magna cum laude in 1943. Those were the war years, and he became a marine fighter pilot in the Pacific theater, flying 120 missions and garnering five medals for bravery.

After returning to civilian life, Pike earned a degree from Columbia University Law School and returned to Riverhead to begin practice. Pike's initial run for public office was not successful, but he was not deterred. He next won two terms as justice of the peace, making him a member of the Riverhead Town Board. As a Democrat, he was elected to the House of Representatives in 1960, unseating an eight-year incumbent Republican, Stuyvesant Wainwright, whom he had challenged two years before. In endorsing Pike for Congress, his hometown newspaper, *The News-Review*, declared, "By natural attributes and by superior training, by grassroots experience and by consistent dedication to the task at hand, Otis Pike personifies the ideal representative at the nation's Capitol for one of the nation's fastest growing, most pivotal geographic areas."

Pike's upset victory in a decidedly Republican stronghold made him a constant target for challengers throughout his nine terms in office. He often said of his eastern Long Island district: "I'm surrounded on three sides by water and on the fourth by Republicans." Pike was repeatedly outspent and outnumbered by his more affluent protagonists. In one notable contest, a barrage of radio advertisements featured a full "God Bless America" chorus. Their rousing voices challenged listeners to do their civic duty with choral waves of patriotism and turn out "the Democrat Pike." Pike countered over the radio with humorous playings of his ukelele that belittled the opposition. He won a resounding victory.

In what has become known as a typical "Pikean" response, a constituent once wrote the congressman to request a favor that Pike declined. The constituent wrote back sarcastically: "Dear Otis, I knew I could count on you." Later, that same letter writer ran for office against Pike. In the closing weeks of the campaign Pike reprinted the "I knew I could count on you" letter in all the local newspapers. Of course, Pike won. Despite skillful but low-budget campaigns, Pike remained invincible to generously bankrolled Republican efforts to unseat him. In an age of nonstop fund-raising, Pike continued to depend on his traditional Long

Island supporters to finance his reelection endeavors, and he proudly proclaimed that he never held a Washington fund-raiser.

From the outset, Pike made it clear he was an unorthodox Democrat. He was more moderate than the rest of the New York delegation, and better understood as an independent man not necessarily bound by party dictates. A fitting description of him might be as a "down-east New Yorker," aligned with a Yankee independence that characterizes the district he so ably represented. His independent political thinking may have stymied his run for the United States Senate in 1968 when he had a passing flirtation with the Democratic nomination. He took his removal from consideration in stride, saying, "I don't know any honorable way of raising two million dollars."

For most of his tenure in the House of Representatives, Pike was a member of the Armed Services Committee. An advocate of a strong national defense, Pike was known for scrapping with generals and admirals and scrupulously questioning their methods. He contrasted President Kennedy's declaration in 1961 that "we will pay any price, bear any burden, meet any hardship, support any friend, oppose any foe to assure the survival and the success of liberty," with Richard Nixon's statement: "[My] central thesis is that the United States will participate in the defense and development of allies and friends, but that America cannot—and will not—conceive all the plans, design all the programs, execute all the defense of the free nations of the world." Pike felt that such contradictions in defense policy contributed to the Pentagon's penchant to always ask for more money.

Although he was a fiscal watchdog to the military, Pike understood the Pentagon's unquenchable thirst for funds, as illustrated by this insightful comment:

> But what's a Joint Chief to do when he doesn't know from one day to the next on what continent he's to be fighting, in defense of what

kind of liberty; whether it will be in a jungle swamp, frozen tundra or high sierra, against sophisticated mechanized armies supported by nuclear weapons, or guerrilla bands armed only with AK-47's? He's going to ask for more, that's what he is going to do.

Pike was quick to define deficiencies when he said the United States armed forces were "larded" with officers and enlisted men whose physical condition was such that their presence contributed more to the military's weakness than to its strength. "We have air conditioned them and inner-springed them and foam-rubbered them and ice creamed them to the point where a 10-mile hike would be an insurmountable burden for far too many of our military," he quipped.

Pike was known as the gadfly member of Congress, eager to ferret out examples of wasteful military spending. He criticized the ratio of officers to enlisted men, lamenting that there were six enlisted men for every officer where formerly there had been seven and a half. He opposed creation of an all-volunteer army, suggesting that increasing military pay to boost recruitment meant sacrificing needed funds for research, development, procurement, and military operations.

In 1967, he made national headlines by exposing large sums of money the Pentagon was spending for small spare parts. That included ten-dollar nuts and fifteen-dollar bolts, available in any hardware store for a few cents. With statements such as, "This is why our military is drowning in fat as well as in paper," Pike successfully forced the Department of Defense to reorganize its buying practices.

Otis Pike is a peerless political pundit whose double-edged wit cuts to the heart of a matter. During a particularly memorable debate in 1973 about flight pay for desk-bound generals, Congressman Pike rose to the floor of the House with arms outstretched, swaying back and forth, conjuring images of an officer in flight with shoulder boards flapping and spinning so fast in his chair as to be propelled out the window. The chamber erupted in laughter, and members voted to defeat the measure. He appropriately, if not irreverently, noted that "everyone is for national defense, particularly when the bucks are spent in their district. No one wants the military to waste money. No one wants a bombing range near him."

In 1975, Pike moved to the House Ways and Means Committee. That same year he also assumed chairmanship of the House Intelligence Committee. His humor helped broker better relations between members of the latter committee after a particularly difficult time of partisan rancor and divisiveness among majority Democrats. In typical Pike style, the congressman wrote a letter to President Ford that enraged White House staffers. His letter noted the return of "a red folder containing . . . highly sensitive material" that was left in Pike's office by a White House counsel. He reassured the president, "If he loses it again, it's okay, I have a copy."

Describing the intricacies of senators and representatives getting together in conference to iron out differences in their bills, Pike said, "Headed by Senator Richard B. Russell and Representative Carl Vinson, both Georgia Democrats, . . . the conferees ended with a figure of $16,976,620,000. A conference is two gentlemen from Georgia talking, arguing, laughing and whispering in each other's ears."

Taking on a new assignment brought this observation:

A couple of weeks ago, by virtue of the facts that I kept breathing and the good people of eastern Long Island were understanding enough to send me back to Congress seven times, I got to be chairman of a subcommittee of the House Armed Services Committee. It has nothing whatsoever to do with talent, a lot to do with the fact that my hair is now white instead of gray, and I breathe rapidly after moderate exercise. It is called the seniority system, and it works. Theoretically, age also improves judgement, but my wife may disagree in my case.

When Secretary of the Interior Rogers C. B. Morton decided to set an example for all Americans by traveling around Washington in a Plymouth Fury to save fuel and limit the use of his official Cadillac limousine to diplomatic functions, Pike opined, "I would like to think that after thus leading the way for all of us by buying another car at taxpayer expense, the Secretary was heard to say, 'I only regret I have but one Cadillac limousine to restrict for my country.'"

Pike has shared this story about being invited to the White House:

I said one of the things which had become a bore after 25 years in politics was the business of being expected to work all day and then go to meetings, receptions or dinners every night. No sooner had that remark been publicized than the invitation came. The President and Mrs. Carter requested the presence of Congressman and Mrs. Pike at dinner on Washington's birthday. Not breakfast. Not a coffee and arm-twisting session. Not a reception or a party. Dinner. Through some inexcusable chain of incompetence in the social secretaries of five separate Presidents over an eighteen year period, the invitation to dinner which all those Presidents surely intended to send, had never reached my desk before. You have had trouble with your mail, too.

Regarding his place at the table, Pike boasted, "Being an avowed social climber I will casually mention the fact that I sat only six feet (six feet, three and a half inches, actually) from the President. I suppose I must also mention that it was from the middle of his back to the middle of mine, for we sat at different tables and faced different directions."

Each year the president submits his annual budget for the

United States to the Congress for consideration. In describing the tradition, Pike once said, "The politics shone through like a bad steak, inadequately covered with onions." His statement remains as true today as it ever was.

Otis Pike put into proper perspective the seriousness of the people's business with the foibles of government and politics. He has been an inspiration to me because he could poke fun not only at others but also at himself. His lighthearted wit is sorely missed in an institution that is all too often defined by strife. Pike decided to retire from public life in January 1979 to pursue his talents as a writer and chronicler of the day. Many of those who know him suspect it also had to do with getting a bit more time for his lifelong loves, boating and fishing.

To this day, he remains a compelling influence in my life. He knew tragedy early, but he never let it get the best of him. He set goals, and when success avoided him, he tried again and was victorious. Pike was focused, was never smitten with himself, and remained close to the people who elected him. When he tired of the hours and saw his patience wane, he took leave of public life.

In the years since Congressman Pike retired, House members have grown more partisan, more divisive, and less charitable to one another. With an abiding sense of fairness as his compass, he needled the federal bureaucracy and injected doses of humor and wit into the most difficult situations, allowing a Congress that rarely smiled to laugh at its own pretentiousness. As we contemplate the arrival of a new millennium, the lessons of his tenure are not lost. The character that Otis Pike personified will serve as a lasting example to all our nation's leaders and decision makers.

CONGRESSMAN
DAVID FUNDERBURK

CONGRESS OF THE UNITED STATES
HOUSE OF REPRESENTATIVES

THE SECOND DISTRICT OF NORTH CAROLINA

Congressman Funderburk is the first Republican to win North Carolina's Second District congressional seat since the beginning of this century. He staunchly supports term limits, a balanced budget, and tougher measures to fight crime.

Funderburk is a former professor, possessing a Ph.D. from the University of South Carolina. He was ambassador to Romania from 1981 to 1985. His political experience is extensive and includes a try for the Republican Senate nomination in 1986. He holds conservative viewpoints regarding foreign aid and domestic social programs that are wasteful of taxpayer dollars.

Funderburk's Second District is a mix of high-growth technology companies in the famed Research Triangle area and the traditional tobacco farming and textile industries in the eastern portion of the district. His conservative views are popular, resulting in a 56 percent vote total for Funderburk in 1994.

Congressman Funderburk lives in Buies Creek with his wife, Betty Jo, and their two children.

Representative Funderburk is a member of the Economic and Educational Opportunities, International Relations, and Small Business Committees. He also serves on eight subcommittees.

How to Contact

427 Cannon House Office Building,
Washington, D.C. 20515
Telephone: 202-225-4531
Fax: 202-225-3191

☆ ☆ ☆ ☆ ☆ ☆ ☆ ☆ ☆ ☆ ☆ ☆ ☆

Only in America could a single mother from the impoverished mountains of North Carolina attend college, work three jobs simultaneously, put four children through college, and have a son who became an ambassador and member of Congress. That very special woman was my mother, Vesta Young Funderburk.

She was born in the beautiful hills of Transylvania County near Brevard, North Carolina. Her profile in character is of a lifelong educator who through hard work, perseverance, and faith in God convinced many people to strive for personal excellence despite all odds. Her message is of encouragement and hope: *the American dream is alive and well inside each individual.* It is also of self-sacrifice and affirmation for the traditional values and strengths of the American family, the backbone of our nation.

Vesta Young grew up in a family of four sisters and one brother. She escaped the deep poverty of the surrounding Appalachian Mountains area by entering Brevard Junior College and then graduating from Western Carolina College with a degree in education. She later completed graduate work in her field of elementary education and lovingly taught for more than three decades in North Carolina schools. Vesta always emphasized the values of a higher education and tapped the individual talents of her students to prepare them for the responsibilities of citizenship.

Vesta was a gifted amateur artist and painted beautiful scenes from nature. Though she possessed other talents, her devotion and dedication were always to her children and education.

Near the end of the devastating depression years, Vesta married Guy B. Funderburk, Ph.D., a South Carolina native, theologian from Baptist Theological Seminary in Louisville, Kentucky, and active Baptist pastor. Dr. Funderburk became the family genealogist and traced his family's roots to the 1720s in western

Germany. He endured the loss of one eye in a childhood accident and overcame this disability to earn a doctorate degree and commission as an army captain and chaplain. During World War II, Captain Funderburk served on a ship in the Pacific theater near the Philippine Islands. Later in the war years and with two daughters in tow, Guy and Vesta were posted to Fort Hood, Texas, then on to Langley Field Army Air Force Base. At the base hospital at Langley Field, in the Hampton Roads area of Virginia, I was born in 1944.

Vesta and Guy divorced when their four children were still very young. I was about five years old. Like so many of today's young mothers, Vesta was forced to make her own way, and she found a teaching position in Aberdeen, North Carolina. In the tiny Sand Hills Community, population 1,600, she made her mark and influenced thousands of students and parents in a positive way. In the 1990s, a single mother with small children is not an unusual occurrence. However, in the 1950s in a little town in North Carolina, that family situation was most unusual.

Vesta was a deeply religious woman who attended church every Sunday and expected her children to do the same and follow the Ten Commandments. In the First Baptist Church of Aberdeen, she was as solid as the pew she occupied. I remember attending Sunday school for six years, without missing a single Sunday, and each year I collected one of those little pins commemorating perfect attendance. I even participated in Bible sword drills that required extensive Bible reading. Of course, Mother greatly encouraged me in those pursuits!

Other than caring for her four children, Mother's first occupation was teaching at Aberdeen Elementary School. She was a very effective teacher—not only because she knew her subjects well, but also because she practiced Dr. Norman Vincent Peale's power of positive thinking. She believed in thinking good thoughts and having faith in oneself. She believed in a work ethic as well. My good friend and a prominent attorney, Richard Craven, recently shared a wonderful story. Richard told me that Vesta helped turn his life around. When he was a bright but unfocused young man and not so self-confident as now, she continually encouraged him. Richard said she was the first person in school to prod him to strive for his best while assuring him he could do it.

She always tried to get the very best out of her students, and many of them, like Richard, gained from her a degree of confidence and a warm encouragement to excel. Many of my former grammar and high school classmates have told me she gave them personal attention and taught that they were valuable as individuals. It was one lesson they have not forgotten.

Vesta became so convinced of the value of the *World Book Encyclopedia* that she assumed a second vocation by selling the sets! On my bedroom wall was a wall-size map of the world. That colorful map aroused my early interest in traveling and in the geographical composition of our planet. I read my *World Books* until I had acquired a rudimentary knowledge about every country they depicted. Years later, as the United States ambassador to Romania, I met and greeted more than one hundred ambassadors from other nations, and I was often astonished that I could call upon my early informal education at home (staring at that enormous map) and recite facts about a particular country, its language, geography, and people.

Mother's third vocation was managing rental homes for an out-of-state owner. I often wondered how she could seemingly spend all her waking moments working without reserving just a little time for her own pleasure. As I grew into adulthood, I realized her enjoyment of life came from working and helping others. She was devoted to her God, her children, her students, and her neighbors and friends. She never missed an opportunity to convince a parent that education was paramount and that the knowledge gained from reading is indispensable. She was very convincing.

Mother convinced me to learn as much about the rest of the world as I could and to always strive for success. My sisters and I were constantly shown that family, home, church, and humility were important. She expected us to prove our worth through hard work. Our ability to strive for excellence—while remembering our roots—has perhaps set us apart later in our lives. To Mother, everyone was equally important in God's eyes. For me, the way we lived at home when I was growing up has been the greatest learning experience of my life.

Vesta succeeded in sending all four of her children to college. I still don't know how she did it all! Gail, her oldest, graduated from the University of North Carolina (UNC) majoring in biology. Judy graduated from Meredith College and majored in English. Betty Dare, the youngest, earned a bachelor's degree from UNC in English and a master's from the University of Virginia. I received B.A. and M.A. degrees in history from Wake Forest University and a Ph.D. at the University of South Carolina. It is no doubt a reflection of Mother's unfaltering belief in education that at one time, all four of her children were teachers.

In 1982, while serving as the ambassador to Romania, I received word in Bucharest that during the night Mother had quietly passed away. She had been alone at her home in Aberdeen. She had planned a trip to Romania in April to see her son in his position as ambassador, but death came a week before her scheduled flight to Bucharest. She had sacrificed so much of herself for her children and others that it seemed a grace from God she was spared prolonged suffering.

Vesta Funderburk's legacy lives on in Aberdeen and in North Carolina. Her personal dedication, motivational skills, and down-to-earth manner influenced thousands. She was a living example of the values and beliefs that knitted the fabric that is America. If her accomplishments were multiplied by applying them to thousands of our citizens, America could be transformed. The work ethic and moral underpinning championed by the Founding Fathers would live today. The family is central to the preservation and stability of our society. Every family must recognize its essential role as it transmits values to the next generation.

My mother taught us to believe in America. During my four-year ambassadorship in Communist Romania, nothing helped me more in understanding and coping with that harsh political environment. As Americans, we were taught that we are blessed among nations and could accomplish anything to which we set our minds. *No* was a word absent from our vocabulary. When I first traveled to Romania as a Fulbright Scholar, complete with wife and child, Mother was concerned for our safety, but she remained supportive.

In the Stalinist Romania of 1971, the people were beaten into submissiveness by a dictatorial police state. Citizens were jailed and persecuted; every detail of their lives was scrutinized. While the ruling elite soothed their anxieties with luxuries unavailable to the masses, ordinary people took out their stored up repressions on each other, at home, at work, and in the streets. In restaurants and businesses operated by the government, those in charge invariably would say, "Nu se poate," meaning it's not possible. Years of oppression stripped them of their religious and cultural heritage, resulting in a way of thinking that was negative and pessimistic about everything. When the Romanian gatekeepers said no, it is not possible, I was able to cut through their stone-faced facade, and I insisted that a positive way to get the job done be found. That is the American ideal. I learned it from Vesta Funderburk.

It is obvious that the most important person in the formative years of my life was my beloved mother, of whom I am very proud. She molded my character, motivated me to strive for the stars, and maintained consistent moral and religious values. She was my total educator.

For most of our American history, public schools promoted individual responsibility and civic virtue. Religion was honored, and lifelong marriage and a stable family were the cornerstones of our democracy. Today, the educational establishment claims moral neutrality but does much to destroy the beliefs of many Americans. Our schools were intended to be places for the intellectual and civic development of our children and not to be places where teachers fear to teach right from wrong. Thomas Jefferson put forward the idea that education should improve the morals of the citizen and provide a structure for the soul.

In education, we have come a long way from the days when my grandparents attended classes and when my mother taught in public schools. We now have birth control clinics inside our schools. Some states require AIDS awareness and homosexual "sensitization training" for children as young as third graders. High school students receive diplomas they cannot read. Surveys indicate that nearly half the students in America test two years below their grade level. All the while, government bureaucrats say they need more money to fix the problems.

I have found that since 1972, federal bureaucrats have spent seventy-six cents out of every dollar on overhead and paperwork, and not on children. The federal government has usurped the role of the parent. No government program, or promise from a politician, can substitute for the values instilled in us by our parents and teachers. As far as I know, government has never raised one child, and it never will. We in the new Congress must get government out of education.

The schools of this nation have a solemn obligation to educate each new generation of Americans not only in math and science but also in the rich heritage and culture of our country, and not bend to each new politically correct idea or pedagogical fad. If the educational establishment is waiting for a wake-up call, its members should listen more closely for the alarm clock. Have they noticed that Americans in large numbers are finally saying, "Enough is enough"? They are racing to in-home schooling and the time-tested results of religion-based educational institutions. Parents are resolutely attempting to reinsert the basics into the education of their children.

Many days I walk through the halls of the Capitol still hardly believing that I am here, a freshman congressman, working in the same place as our nation's forefathers. It is humbling, and I am grateful for the opportunity. To be a servant to the people of my state is a monumental personal responsibility. I am committed to preserving our American freedoms and to downsizing the federal government so that all Americans may fulfill their dreams and reach their greatest potential.

As an educator like my mother, I have lived the American dream. Every day I am thankful that I was born in the USA and was wonderfully blessed to have such a mother and mentor. I was taught in Luke 12:48 that "to whom much is given, from him much will be required." Yes, each of us can make a difference! One by one, in his or her own place. It is our responsibility to preserve this great nation for our children and grandchildren. My mother did it for me, I know you can do it, too.

Translated into English, Gutknecht means "good hired hand." Exemplifying that description, Congressman Gutknecht worked his way through college at a school supply and equipment company. Upon graduation, he was hired by the company as an outside salesperson. He traveled the First District for ten years in that capacity. In 1978, Gutknecht graduated from Auction College. He is a licensed real estate broker and auctioneer. He still does fund-raising auctions.

First elected to public office in 1982, Gutknecht served six terms in the Minnesota House of Representatives. In 1992, he was elected floor leader for the Minnesota House Republican Caucus. He won the 1994 First District congressional seat with 55 percent of the vote.

Representative Gutknecht's nonpolitical interests include college basketball, the stock market, fishing, and outdoor sports. He lives in Rochester with his wife, Mary, and their three children, Margie, Paul, and Emily.

Congressman Gutknecht serves on the Government Reform and Oversight Committee and the Science Committee. He is a member of six subcommittees.

How to Contact

425 Cannon House Office Building,
Washington, D.C. 20515
Telephone: 202-225-2472
Fax: 202-225-3246

☆ ☆ ☆ ☆ ☆ ☆ ☆ ☆ ☆ ☆ ☆ ☆ ☆ ☆

About a dozen years ago, as a new member of the state legislature and a visitor to our state capital for only the third time, I took the interesting and informative tour of the capitol building offered by the Minnesota Historical Society. Although I don't remember many details, I will never forget my stop at the simple plaque on the wall of the rotunda.

It told the story of a Civil War colonel, William Colvill, and the First Minnesota Regiment. It is a tale of personal sacrifice and courage. The story is even more meaningful because it is absolutely true. Its message burned deeply into me, and I am pleased to share it with you now.

By any measure, William Colvill was a giant. He stood nearly six feet five inches tall and was of large frame. When the Confederates launched the first battle of the Civil War by firing on Fort Sumter in Charleston harbor, Minnesota governor Alexander Ramsey happened to be in Washington on other business. He raced to the White House to become the first governor to volunteer troops for the Union army. A few nights later, in Red Wing, Minnesota, William Colvill used his considerable size and agility to elbow his way to the front of a line and become the first volunteer in the first regiment of the first state that volunteered to support the Union.

James A. Wright, in his historical epic documentary *The Story of Company F*, gave this account of Colvill: "William Colvill was a lawyer, a Democrat and the editor of the *Red Wing Sentinel*, born in New York and about thirty years old. I do not know how it happened that he was the choice for captain, as I am sure that the majority of the company were Republicans, but I presume that the question of party politics did not enter into the case." Despite his political affiliation, Colvill was fiercely loyal to the Union and to "the boys in the First Regiment."

Minnesota's First Regiment fought with distinction in many

of the bloodiest battles of the Civil War including Fredericksburg, Bull Run, and Antietam. American history has a special footnote to commemorate their actions on July 2, 1863, in that most famous of Civil War contests, the Battle of Gettysburg. What was about to become the longest day of the war began early for the Minnesotans. Isaac Taylor of the First Regiment recorded in his diary, "Aroused at 3:00 a.m. and ordered to pack up, and at 4:00 a.m. move towards the battlefield where we arrived at 5:40 a.m. Order from General Gibbon read to us in which he says that this is to be the great battle of the war and that any soldier leaving the ranks without leave will be instantly put to death."

On the long, hot march from Washington into Pennsylvania, Colvill had sided with his men and ignored orders by allowing them to remove their boots while crossing a creek. Because of that seemingly innocent act, he was facing a potential court-martial when hostilities commenced at Gettysburg. He rejoined his regiment on July 2. The First was positioned somewhat south of the middle of the long Union line on Cemetery Ridge. New Yorkers under the command of General Sickles had moved about a mile forward into a peach orchard. The movement left an unnoticed, but huge, gap in the Union line. The Confederates, always quick to recognize a weakness, seized upon the opportunity and launched an offensive against Sickles's isolated position and the gap in the line.

General Winfield Scott Hancock was commanding the Union forces. Nicknamed "The Superb," he was among the best of Lincoln's field generals, and he enjoyed unquestioned respect from his troops. Hancock saw the vulnerability of the Union position about the same time as his Confederate counterparts, who were already pressing against the weakest portion of the Union line. Hancock rode to Colvill and nervously asked how long he could hold the position. Colvill, who usually spoke in short, crisp sentences, firmly answered, "General, to the last man." It was no idle boast and proved to be prophetic. That single phrase survives today as the motto of the Minnesota National Guard detachment that traces its heritage to the Minnesota First Regiment.

Later, as the Union situation became more desperate, Hancock knew that he needed time to bring up reserves and reorganize the Union defense, but first he needed to slow the Confederate advance. Hancock ordered the First Regiment to counterattack, directly into the teeth of the Confederate charge. Colvill calmly ordered his men to fix bayonets, close ranks, and head down the hill. They were outnumbered at least four to one. Colvill had watched the battle evolve and understood that Hancock's order would mean heavy casualties, but he didn't flinch because he knew the outcome of that pivotal battle hung in the balance.

It was dusk when Colvill began the counterattack. The Minnesota boys were quickly enveloped on three sides by battle-tested Alabama infantry. Confederate rifles thinned the ranks of the Minnesotans, but on they went. Grapeshot and shrapnel tore through the human wall, lining the path to the Confederates with Union bodies. The charge picked up speed as it neared a small dried-out creek bed. A survivor, Company F's Sergeant Lochren, told what it was like: "Charge!, shouted Colvill as we neared their first line; and with leveled bayonets at full speed, we rushed upon it. The men were never made who will stand against leveled bayonets coming with momentum and evident desperation. The first line broke, stopping the whole advance." Lochren continued to describe the action: "Our men fall, many pierced by balls both from the right side and front. We fire away three, four, five irregular volleys and but little ammunition is wasted when muzzles of opposing guns almost meet."

Sergeant Lochren added after the battle,

It is hard for us now to imagine the horrors of that day. The Confederate charge had been stopped and both sides withdrew as night fell over the battlefield. It was then that the bodies were retrieved and counted. The Regiment had stopped the enemy and held back its mighty force and saved the position. But at what sacrifice! Nearly every officer was dead or lay weltering with bloody wounds, our gallant Colonel and every field officer among them. Of the two-hundred and sixty-two men who made the charge, two-hundred and fifteen lay upon the field, stricken down by rebel bullets, forty-seven were still in line, and not a man was missing. The annals of war contain no parallel to this charge. In its desperate valor, complete execution, successful result, and in its sacrifice of men in proportion to the number engaged, authentic history has no record with which it can be compared.

The Minnesotans suffered an incredible 82 percent casualty rate, the highest percentage of casualties of any Union regiment in any battle of the Civil War. General Hancock solemnly explained the reason for his order that had visited so much destruction on the First Regiment: "There is no more gallant deed recorded in history. I ordered because I saw I must gain five minutes time. I would have ordered that regiment in if I had known that every man would be killed. It had to be done and I was glad to find such a gallant body of men at hand willing to make the sacrifice that the occasion demanded."

The men of Minnesota's First made many gallant sacrifices throughout the war. When the regiment headed off to war in 1861, they were 1,023 strong. After Pickett's charge at Gettysburg had been repelled by the Union stand, only two years later, just 67 men could report for duty.

Although twice wounded in the foot and shoulder, Colvill survived his wounds and the Civil War. The injuries caused him to walk with a cane the rest of his life and endure considerable pain. He was not slowed by his disabilities. Colvill became the state attorney general, practiced law, and was the editor of a newspaper in Red Wing. Later in life, when asked what he thought about as he led his regiment full speed down the hill at Gettysburg, Colvill replied, "Gad! I thought of Washington!" Colvill remained active in public affairs until the day he died in his sleep at the Soldiers' Home in Saint Paul. He was preparing to lead his men once more, that time to the dedication of the new state capitol building.

A visit by a president to a small town in middle America is still a major event. In the days when rail transportation dominated travel it was an event that brought people great distances to witness. In July 1928, President and Mrs. Calvin Coolidge came by train to tiny Cannon Falls, Minnesota, to dedicate a monument to William Colvill. The president's participation in honoring his bravery underscored our nation's appreciation for the colonel.

On that warm summer day, normally "Silent Cal" passionately praised Colonel Colvill and the Minnesota First Regiment:

> In all the history of warfare, the charge at Gettysburg has few, if any, equals and no superiors. It was an exhibition of the most exalted heroism against an apparently insuperable antagonist. Holding the Confederate forces in check until other reserves came up, it probably saved the Union Army from defeat. What that defeat would have meant to the North, no one can tell. Washington, Philadelphia, New York and the whole North would have been lost. So far as human judgement can determine, Colonel Colvill, and those eight companies of the Minnesota First, are entitled to rank among the saviors of their country.

I tell the story of Colonel William Colvill and the Minnesota First to many of my audiences. When I was in the state legislature, I encouraged every visitor to read that simple plaque. Many did, and all were moved by it. I share this story because I think we owe something to those brave young men. They believed this nation was worth fighting for; they believed America was worth dying for.

Fighting for what we believe can be a thankless and frustrating task, but it's seldom fatal. We live in a nation that is both free and united thanks to their selfless contribution. To remember their sacrifice is to make our burden seem light by comparison. We owe them no less than our very best effort, and the debt can be repaid only by our never-ending rededication to preserving this "last best hope of man on earth," this America.

**CONGRESSMAN
JOHN HOSTETTLER**

CONGRESS OF THE UNITED STATES

HOUSE OF REPRESENTATIVES

THE EIGHTH DISTRICT OF INDIANA

Representative Hostettler, a political newcomer, unseated a six-term Democratic incumbent to win his district's congressional seat with 52 percent of the vote.

Hostettler's legislative priorities are cutting taxes for the middle class, reducing the taxation and regulation for business, and making Congress more open to public scrutiny. He also supports a strong national defense.

The Wadesville resident is a mechanical engineer who took a leave of absence from the Southern Indiana Gas & Electric Company to campaign. Hostettler states his professional experience will help shape his political life.

Congressman Hostettler is a graduate of the Rose-Hulman Institute of Technology and is a registered professional engineer. He is married to the former Elizabeth Ann Hamman. They have three children, Matthew, Amanda, and Jaclyn.

Representative Hostettler is a member of the National Security and Agriculture Committees and serves on several subcommittees.

How to Contact

> 1404 Longworth Office Building,
> Washington, D.C. 20515
> Telephone: 202-225-4636
> Fax: 202-225-3294

☆ ☆ ☆ ☆ ☆ ☆ ☆ ☆ ☆ ☆ ☆ ☆ ☆ ☆

During the first century, the apostle Paul's letter to the church in Rome acknowledged the persecutions inflicted against Christians by the government and encouraged the brethren to persevere: "But we also glory in tribulations, knowing that tribulation produces perseverance" (Rom. 5:3).

William Wilberforce, a member of the British Parliament during the late eighteenth and early nineteenth centuries, and generally credited with ending the English slave trade, exemplified many noble virtues during his lifetime. Compassion, service, and integrity come immediately to mind. By examining the whole of his life, I find the virtue that was consistent in all his planning, actions, and deeds was perseverance.

Wilberforce's lifelong application of perseverance is especially noteworthy because it worked for him not only in special occasions but also in three critical areas of his life. He persevered because of his deep faith in God; he persevered for the sake of fellow human beings instead of himself; and he persevered against institutionalized opposition from other members of Parliament and the entrenched resistance of wealthy Britons who felt their pockets would be picked if Wilberforce's ideas became law.

Wilberforce did not choose small projects when his personal beliefs set him on the road to becoming a political reformer. "God almighty has set before me two great objects," he exhorted early in his parliamentary career, "the suppression of the slave trade and the reformation of manners." In Wilberforce's day, "manners" meant morals, an area of English life he considered greatly insufficient.

William Wilberforce was born in August 1759, in Hull, England, the son of a wealthy merchant. He was elected to Parliament in 1780 at the age of twenty-one. His early rise to a seat in the national legislature is one common experience we share. Though separated in time by more than two hundred years, our common interest in wide-scale government reform and our willingness to take a stand based on moral principle rather than political expediency are prominent mutual causes. Someday, I pray my eulogy will proclaim that perseverance was another shared trait.

Wilberforce saw the low spiritual awareness of the English as the breeding ground of tolerance to slavery. Moreover, he recognized the lucrative profits from trading in slaves were fueling the ruling elite's apathy toward the plight of hundreds of thousands of human beings whose entire lives were spent in chains. If the slave trade could be outlawed, and its profits gone, there would be little support for slavery as an institution. Although Wilberforce's efforts seemed to be concentrated on ending the slave trade, he knew if he were successful, the death of slavery was sure to follow. Wilberforce set out on a decades-long journey that targeted slavery as an evil to be blotted out. He sensed that a greater evil must be lying beneath the surface of his society to foster such a heinous institution, and the societal cause that allowed slavery to exist must be addressed.

While visiting the Continent in 1784–85, Wilberforce became a Christian and launched his mission to repeal the laws that allowed the slave trade. The two events were definitely related. Upon his conversion and acceptance of Christ, given politics' traditional familiarity with impropriety, Wilberforce at first considered retirement from public life, but he decided instead to try to make a difference by working vigorously from his new vantage point of Christian love for his fellow human beings.

Predictably, opposition to Wilberforce's first attempt to end the slave trade was vehement. Some simply feared change; others were indignant when they recognized the move as an indictment of their willingness to cooperate with such an evil institution. Of course, the "low visibility" reason for most of the opposition was the deep financial stake in slaves held by many high-ranking

British individuals as well as the monetary value of the slave trade to the total British economy. Wilberforce wanted to gore everybody's ox, a most unpopular course of action.

Wilberforce did not recklessly attack the entrenched establishment. A frontal assault was not his style. Instead, he offered to turn the other cheek. "I mean not to accuse anyone," he lamented in a speech before Parliament, "but to take the shame upon myself, in common indeed with the whole Parliament of Britain, for having suffered this horrid trade to be carried on under their authority. We are all guilty, we ought all to plead guilty, and not exculpate ourselves by throwing the blame on others."

Despite Wilberforce's eloquent arguments and the support of such powerful allies as M.P. Edmund Burke and Prime Minister William Pitt, the proponents of continuing the slave trade used procedural gimmicks to forestall the abolition. The effort might be akin to using a filibuster in our modern Senate. Of course, like today, the most common tactic was to banish the proposal to the black hole of some committee, never to be seen again. The issue was kept in committee four years before it was defeated in 1791 by a 163 to 88 vote. In those raucous times, members of Parliament frequently bought their seats, and the same brokers who controlled sections of Parliament controlled the slave trade.

No matter how eloquent the arguments or numerous the petitions for abolition, the guardians of the institution that traded human lives for money showed the depth of their corruption by voting against Wilberforce's measure. Wilberforce persevered. Further votes were brought to the floor of the House of Commons in 1793 and 1794; every year from 1796 through 1799; and in 1804 and 1805. Support for anti–slave trading laws grew to the point that in 1804 the measure actually passed the House of Commons, but was defeated in the House of Lords.

By that time, Wilberforce's opponents should have been getting his message that he was not going to quit. He never seemed to doubt that he would eventually win. That his motivation stemmed in part from his Christian beliefs is made clear in his writings. Wilberforce explained his conviction by stating,

> In the present instance, where the actual commission of guilt is in question, a man who fears God is not at liberty. To you I will say a strong thing which the motive I have suggested will both explain and justify. If I thought that the immediate Abolition of the Slave Trade would cause an insurrection in our islands, I should not for an instant remit my most serious endeavors. Be persuaded then, I shall still even less make this grand cause the sport of caprice, or sacrifice it to motives of political convenience or personal feeling.

No less a figure than the English evangelist and founder of the Methodist movement in mid-nineteenth-century England, John Wesley, writing shortly before his death, identified Wilberforce's faith as playing the central role in his drive to abolish the slave trade. Wesley cautioned, "Unless God has raised you up for this very thing, you will be worn out by the opposition of men and devils; but if God is with you, who can be against you? Are all of them stronger than God? Oh, be not weary in well-doing. Go on, in the name of God and in the power of His might, till even American slavery, the vilest that ever saw the sun, shall vanish away before it."

Wilberforce's compassion for his fellow human beings, regardless of color, was self-evident. The very fact that he wished to abolish the slave trade, and slavery itself, revealed his understanding of its wickedness. In his speeches he often detailed the deplorable conditions of the slave ships, the despicable misery visited upon slaves sent to the colonies, and the invisible emotional wounds inflicted upon families, both before and after they were kidnapped into slavery.

Because the forces supporting slavery were so enmeshed in

British society and commerce, Wilberforce needed to persevere for an incredible twenty years before he saw his efforts rewarded. It also meant slave families were subjected to almost unimaginable treatment for another twenty years. That Wilberforce succeeded in erasing the slave trade does not blot out its horrible smear on the record of humankind. In 1807, Wilberforce's motion finally carried by an overwhelming margin, leading to a similar attempt in the United States eight months later. That started the dominoes falling, although there was still much suffering from slavery around the world. It was not to fully end until the conclusion of the American Civil War in 1865. Perseverance had brought about the triumph of William Wilberforce's cause.

Simultaneously, Wilberforce was facing a similar ordeal in his drive for the reformation of manners in Britain. In his day, again, "manners" referred to the moral fabric of his nation and its people. Because Wilberforce viewed his country's spiritual decadence as the cause of so many social ills, he considered this challenge the more important of the two. He believed that if the moral will of the people and their leaders had upheld the tenets of their Christian faith, slavery would never have been established, much less have prospered.

The Great Awakening that swept through England's lower and middle classes in the latter eighteenth century had sprung from a desperate culture, steeped in violence, infidelity, and apathy toward social problems. The upper class and the nation's official institutions remained largely unmoved by the work of George Whitefield, an enthusiastic evangelist, and other religious reformers. The moneyed aristocracy looked with particular disdain at the evangelical movement and ascribed to it a label of mindless emotionalism, much as some people do today.

Rather than railing in return, Wilberforce, true to his logic, saw the public cynicism as an outward symptom of an inner spiritual vacuum. The spiritual void hurt the country in many ways. He hoped to improve the quality of British life by instilling a greater respect for law and authority and a return to, dare I say it, family values! Wilberforce's perseverance was directed to support a proclamation made by King George III at Wilberforce's behest. It was titled "Proclamation for the Encouragement of Piety and Virtue and for the Preventing of Vice, Profanities and Immorality." Although a bit restrictive for today's readers, in the early nineteenth century it spawned the formation of hundreds of local societies dedicated to carrying out its decree. There followed a flurry of published material that was widely distributed and widely read.

Garth Lean's book *God's Politician* cited three scholars' accounts of the effect Wilberforce's efforts to reform morals had on the English people. Professor Henry Perkins, in his *Origins of Modern Society*, wrote, "Between 1780 and 1850 the English ceased to be one of the most aggressive, brutal, rowdy, outspoken, riotous, cruel and bloodthirsty nations in the world; and became one of the most inhibited, polite, orderly, tender-minded, prudish and critical." Scholar David Newsome rated evangelism as "perhaps the most formative power behind the eminence of the most eminent Victorians" and Edward Stokes described this vignette of English history as "the rock upon which the character of the nineteenth century Englishman was founded."

Because Wilberforce saw the amelioration of manners as the greater of the two tasks he was bent on accomplishing, some of his enemies were cut more severely by this less-obvious goal than by the drive against slavery. Despite the rumormongering aimed at assassinating his character, Wilberforce persevered. Again his deep-rooted faith provided the inner strength to do so.

Garth Lean explained,

Certainly too, that reliance, through good and ill, on a wise God, lay at the root of Wilberforce's serenity. He did all that he could and then left the result in the hands of God. Otherwise, he could not have survived so many disappointments. His faith was resilient because it was not in himself, but as he said after one of his defeats, in God "who has given the very small increase there has been so far and must give all, if there be more."

William Wilberforce's unselfish example of unending effort to better his society must be emulated if we are to accomplish needed reforms in our own time.

His tribulations and eventual victory can be instructive to us in many ways. First, he displayed remarkable perseverance during agonizing decades of defeat. He never wavered from his task. He had a clear purpose and a key goal to accomplish, the abolition of the slave trade. As a public figure, he consistently espoused the reformation of morals. It is interesting to me, as a freshman legislator in the 104th Congress, to recognize that Wilberforce knew the social maladies of his day had as their foundation root causes that were beyond his reach as a legislator. He sought to abolish the dominant moral issue of his era, slavery; but he poured his passion into solving the underlying cause of not only slavery, but all vice. That is, the creation of virtue.

Wilberforce was irreversibly committed to his principles and did not allow repeated setbacks to dissuade him. He was not afraid to fight against institutionalized opposition in Parliament. He was not overly concerned with his own popularity; he went about his duty in a way that earned respect and appreciation for his cause from colleagues and the public. An unapologizing personal faith powered his ideas about issues, and he was motivated to action by a desire to improve the lives of his fellow human beings.

America needs thousands of William Wilberforces today. We need them in Congress and the executive branch. We need them on our judicial benches. We need their presence in the media, law enforcement, education, medicine, and the legal profession. We need to hear their voices in community leadership, in places of worship and, even more than all of these, in our homes and with our families. We need Americans who will take a stand for that to which Providence has called us, who are motivated by faith and an unselfish desire to improve the lot of their fellow human beings. We need citizens who will look to the long-term positive growth of our society rather than short-term expediency.

Great are the odds against reforming our society, but William Wilberforce has shown us how and proven beyond any doubt that one person can make a difference. America's cries for help include battling the acceptance of morals of convenience, increased disregard for human life, runaway crime rates, irresponsible spending of the public money by a tax-and-spend bureaucracy, and abandonment of public trust in our political institutions.

I have made a personal commitment to follow in Wilberforce's footsteps. To that end, I will use any manner of public forum available to me to affect the manners and morals of my fellow citizens. I shall stand for principle above politics, faith above crassness, compassion above apathy. And I shall persevere, with God's help.

CONGRESSMAN
STEVE LARGENT

CONGRESS OF THE UNITED STATES
HOUSE OF REPRESENTATIVES

THE FIRST DISTRICT OF OKLAHOMA

Many people knew Steve Largent as a record-setting pass receiver in the National Football League. In fourteen years with the Seattle Seahawks, Largent set six career records and participated in seven Pro Bowls. In July 1995, he was inducted into the Pro Football Hall of Fame.

Since retiring from the NFL in 1989, Largent has operated an advertising and marketing consulting firm. Largent's commitment to young people is well known, as is his service to charitable causes throughout his community and the nation. He serves on the advisory board of the Tulsa area Salvation Army and has served on the board of trustees of the University of Tulsa. He remains active with the Fellowship of Christian Athletes and Focus on the Family, a Christian ministry.

Representative Largent is a native of Tulsa and graduated from the University of Tulsa in 1976. He and his wife, Terry, have a daughter, Casie, and three sons, Kyle, Kelly, and Kramer.

Largent is a member of the Budget, Science, and Commerce

Committees and serves on several subcommittees and the Health Care Task Force.

How to Contact

> 410 Cannon House Office Building,
> Washington, D.C. 20515
> Telephone: 202-225-2211

☆ ☆ ☆ ☆ ☆ ☆ ☆ ☆ ☆ ☆ ☆ ☆ ☆

After spending fourteen years as a pass receiver in the National Football League, I am convinced that the arena of professional sports is not necessarily the place to look for humility and generosity. With so many of our young college athletes focusing at least one eye on the prestige and high income provided by a major sports franchise, it is reassuring to discover a fine young athlete who already possesses these qualities.

My choice for a profile in character is my fellow Oklahoman, Scott Pierce. Scott's determination and devotion to his sport would be enough to make him a candidate for this chapter. But what made Scott Pierce a champion as a human being as well as an athlete was what happened after his championship basketball experience culminated.

When Pierce arrived at Oklahoma State University for the fall semester in 1992, his new teammates had told him about Scott Carter, describing him as "this brave little guy." OSU's basketball team had made Scott Carter, from my hometown of Tulsa, an honorary member in 1991. He was only twelve years old at the time and was recovering from the first of many spinal and lung operations to try to stop a cancer from spreading throughout his body.

Pierce commented, "I remember that they said Coach Eddie Sutton considered Scott Carter a member of the OSU basketball family." As a transfer student from the University of Illinois in 1992, Pierce was not eligible to play that season, but he sat on the bench with the OSU team alongside Scott Carter. Carter continued to occupy a special place on the Cowboys' bench until his death in 1993.

While they sat on a bench at courtside, neither one able to play, a personal bond was formed, and Scott Pierce and Scott Carter became friends. Pierce marveled at how Carter never complained about his setbacks, maintaining his upbeat attitude as he joked with OSU players during visits to the team dressing room. Pierce and his teammates also became close to the young Carter's parents and visited their home in Tulsa for Thanksgiving weekend in 1993.

The last time Scott Pierce saw the ailing Carter was the Thanksgiving weekend when OSU opened the season by defeating Providence College in Tulsa. By then, Carter was seriously ill with a brain tumor. Pierce tells how "we went to see him and he was very sick. But he came to our next game and we later learned it was with a temperature of 104 degrees."

Six days later, the Cowboys defeated Arizona State in a nationally televised game. It was their most impressive performance of the new basketball season, and afterward they celebrated back in their hotel room. Unknown to the players, Scott Carter, less than a week away from his fourteenth birthday, had died while the game was being played. "Coach Sutton called us into a meeting," Pierce sadly recalls, "shortly after we arrived at the hotel. He had tears in his eyes, which is very uncharacteristic of Sutton. I knew right away something had happened. He told us Scott Carter had died. You could hear a pin drop. One moment we had been so happy about winning and the next moment we were solemn."

That was a Friday night, and the OSU team had to leave the next morning to play the University of Arizona in Tucson on Sunday. The entire team flew home Sunday night after the game to attend Scott Carter's funeral on Monday. While the whole team mourned the loss of their friend, Pierce sought to prolong his memory by displaying the young man's photograph prominently in his dorm room.

Later in his college year, Pierce was not doing well as a reserve player. He was a relatively obscure player on the Oklahoma State basketball team, garnering little attention and having no strong presence on the court. The young hoopster was already experiencing the frustrations that a more seasoned player might face. Pierce remembers that "he looked at Carter's picture and wondered how Scott, with all his pain, could always be happy." Honestly admitting that he felt guilty about feeling sorry for himself, Pierce extols, "Scott inspired me to give a better effort. That's when everything got better for me."

A broken hand in his junior year had sidelined him once, and then, unbelievably, it happened again. A second broken hand soured the beginning of his senior season in college basketball. It was his final year on the team and his last chance to prove his mettle, but his future looked bleak. Pierce persevered, and by midseason his determination to overcome physical problems and become a first-string player had paid off. Pierce was in the limelight as a pivotal player who excelled at defense and rebounding. His promotion to the starting lineup coincided with the start of OSU's 17–3 record that would carry them to the Final Four, the championship series, in Seattle. Pierce's inspired and rejuvenated playing had helped the OSU Cowboys in their quest to reach the Final Four.

Pierce played what many consider the best game of his college career in the NCAA East Final against the University of Massachusetts. That game not only earned Pierce a coveted slot on the All-East tournament team, but also inspired his teammates and fans to make Pierce the team's symbol, a sort of mascot. Scott Pierce had lost a tooth during an especially physical part of the game against UMASS, and soon "Toothless in Seattle" T-shirts featuring Scott's smiling face could be found everywhere. They sold by the thousands at the Final Four.

After his winning season at OSU, Scott Pierce spoke of his admiration for Scott Carter at the Cowboys' postseason banquet. Pierce told how the photo of Carter that he kept in his room had been taken shortly before Carter's death. "He was shooting a basketball and I was in the background. After he died, his parents gave me the picture. I kept it on my desk where I could always see it. I remember I was looking at it one night when I was pretty down and feeling sorry for myself. Then, I realized how petty I was to be complaining, when Scott never complained about all that he went through, even when his leg was amputated. I made a commitment to quit moaning and give basketball my best effort. The remainder of the season was great for the team and me, after that."

Although the banquet is the proud event when the winning players receive their personalized Final Four rings, Pierce made no mention of the plans he had made for his ring. He would donate it to Scott Carter's parents, to be displayed by a foundation that exhibits memorabilia of their son's sports heroes to raise funds for cancer research. Pierce saved his humble gesture of love and generosity for Carter's parents without a trace of fanfare or publicity. It was a warm and exceptional expression of respect for his friend who had been a source of inspiration to him, the OSU team, and the people of Oklahoma.

The handsome six-nine youth originally from Euless, Texas, displayed a manly sense of respect and honor for another by giving away what would surely be the most cherished possession of any college basketball player, his hard-earned Final Four championship ring. Scott Pierce donated the circular trophy of his greatest accomplishment to the parents of another young basketball player he had loved and admired, Scott Carter.

Mike and his wife, Paula, were overwhelmed with emotion and deep appreciation for the selfless act of generosity that Scott Pierce displayed in parting with his ring, and they expressed sincere regret that Pierce would not have it to enjoy as the years passed. Scott Pierce's act of generosity was not impulsive. He had explained to his father, "I was going to give my Final Four ring to the Carters because it was something I wanted to do, because of what Scott and his family meant to me. I thought it would mean a lot to Scott. And it meant a lot to me to do it." Pierce continued by recounting his blessings: "A lot of wonderful things happened to me because I went to Oklahoma State University. As I reflect, the best things happened because of Scott and his parents, all of whom knew Christ. And my basketball career turned around because of Scott Carter."

There are about 3,600 Division I college basketball players, and they all dream of earning a Final Four ring. Only forty-five to fifty players will receive this cherished icon in any given year, making it among the most rare and sought-after awards a college athlete may receive. With a Final Four ring come well-deserved recognition and respect from sporting peers. These are attributes Scott Pierce could never give away; they are his forever.

To those who believe it is better to give than to receive, there is indeed good news in store, both on earth and in heaven! For Scott Pierce, his good fortune had already begun, and with God willing, it will most likely follow him to heaven as well. Unknown to anyone, the manufacturer of the Final Four rings had determined that of all the rings made that year, two of them were not up to standard. Being a reputable company, it produced two new rings and sent them to OSU coach Eddie Sutton. Like the originals, the replacements were personalized and bore the names of two players, Jason Skaer, and yes, Scott Pierce!

Coach Sutton had not seen the replacements until shortly before the awards banquet and had intended to give them to the parents of Skaer and Pierce, but he did not have the opportunity to do so. After learning Pierce had given his ring to the Carter family, Coach Sutton decided to personally give the new ring to him. Pierce was summoned to Sutton's office the day after he gave his ring to the Carters: "I had no idea why he wanted to see me. When I walked into the room, he tossed the replacement ring to me. I thought the Carters had wanted me to have the original, after all. It was not until the next day when I asked Coach Sutton more questions that he told me about the replacement ring the manufacturer had sent. There were only two, and one of them had my name on it! It was unbelievable!" Coach Sutton exclaimed to Pierce, "The Lord works in mysterious ways!"

Pierce reveals, "I was not a Christian when I met Scott, but I thought a lot about what it was that enabled Scott and his parents to be so positive throughout their tremendous adversity. Finally, I realized it was because they knew the Lord. When I became a Christian, I found the same contentment. Scott was a gift from God. My experience with the Carters was a gift from God. I wear the replacement ring because I consider it a gift from God." The Carters have assured Pierce that the original ring will never be sold and will be returned to him if he ever wants it back.

Scott Pierce recently declined an offer to play for a professional team in Taiwan. He graduates in the spring of 1996. Then he is looking forward to being a science teacher and, of course, a coach.

Scott Pierce has a Final Four ring that proves he has been a very special athlete, but the Scott Carter family has a Final Four ring that proves Scott Pierce is a very special human being, possessing extraordinary character.

CONGRESSMAN
RON LEWIS

CONGRESS OF THE UNITED STATES
HOUSE OF REPRESENTATIVES

THE SECOND DISTRICT OF KENTUCKY

Representative Lewis got a head start on his 1994 freshmen GOP colleagues by winning a special election in May 1994. The victory sent him to Congress to replace the late Representative William Natcher, a Democrat who had held the congressional seat for forty years. Lewis is the first Republican in more than a century to represent this part of Kentucky.

After winning the special election with 55 percent of the vote, Lewis triumphed again in the November general election, this time winning 60 percent of the votes cast.

Lewis signed the Republican Contract with America, and he supports term limits, a balanced budget amendment, lower taxes, and a smaller federal government.

Congressman Lewis attended Moorehead State University and the University of Kentucky and holds a bachelor's degree and a master's degree. He is a Baptist minister and the former owner of a religious bookstore. Lewis and his wife, Kayi, and their two children reside in Elizabethtown, Kentucky.

Lewis's Second District is very competitive politically, and more than two-thirds of the voters are registered as Democrats. These independent-minded constituents extend from the southwest Kentucky hill country, to Louisville on the north, and the Bluegrass region in the east.

Representative Lewis is a member of the Agriculture and National Security Committees. He also serves on four subcommittees.

How to Contact

412 Cannon House Office Building,
Washington, D.C. 20515
Telephone: 202-225-3501

☆ ☆ ☆ ☆ ☆ ☆ ☆ ☆ ☆ ☆ ☆ ☆ ☆

In 1946, Americans longed to address their pressing domestic concerns and recover from the exhaustion of World War II. The shortages and rationing of the war postponed most personal decisions, but after the war, there were homes to be built, cars to be bought, and families to be raised. I spent much of my childhood during the postwar years in the tiny eastern Kentucky town of Southshore. I may be the only member of this Congress who was born in a real log cabin!

When my father took a job in Ashland, Kentucky, I attended public school and through its traditional teachings and local folklore began to learn the legend of Henry Clay. My interest in Clay was piqued by the fact that my adopted hometown of Ashland is also the name of Clay's two-hundred-acre home in Lexington, Kentucky. Today, nearly 150 years after his death in 1852, you can visit his Ashland estate and the memorial Henry Clay High School just a mile or so away. Clay's tomb can be seen for miles as it rises above the trees in historic Lincoln Cemetery, not far from his beloved Ashland.

As a young man, Henry Clay left his native Virginia to travel the Wilderness Road to Kentucky. Clay called Kentucky home for the rest of his life, save for his frequent trips to Washington, D.C. The astonishing rise of Clay's career would be the envy of any modern statesman: an attorney at the age of twenty; Speaker of the House of Representatives for a total of six terms, the first term coming unbelievably as a thirty-three-year-old freshman congressman; one of five United States peace commissioners at the Treaty of Ghent; secretary of state; United States senator; and presidential candidate for both Whig and Republican Parties.

As a child, I found he was a great orator, and I imagined that he needed to be so that his voice could be heard beyond the hills. I was then too young to know he was the leader of the War Hawks, a group that espoused military preparedness as a deterrent to aggressors, and author of the Compromise of 1850 that purposed to stave off the bloody American Civil War that consumed our nation a few years after his death. Nor did I know that when he was a young boy of my age, British horsemen during the Revolutionary War had driven their swords into his father's fresh grave, looking for war booty. The callous act was finally ended by the frantic appeals of Clay's widow. Young Henry Clay watched the scene in horror, "with eyes that never forgot." He was later to say of his childhood, "Rocked in the cradle of the Revolution . . . , I was born a Democrat and raised and nurtured a Republican."

Clay's affinity for a republican form of government began early. He wanted a government that would forever protect his country and his fellow citizens from the tyranny of brutal oppression. Clay found the antidote to tyranny in the principles of a free government of the people, laid down by the Founding Fathers and articulated by Publius in the *Federalist* papers. When Clay went to Washington in the early 1800s, our federal government had existed for only a few decades. Just as Clay was nurtured a Republican, so too, did he nurture his republic.

Publius defined a *republic* as "a government which derives all its powers directly or indirectly from the great body of the people, and is administered by persons holding their offices during pleasure for a limited period, or during good behavior." Clay agreed with this definition but also realized that the great body of the people can be both the cause and the cure for factional discords that pull at the seams of all democratic governments. Dissenters are a necessary hindrance in any majoritarian government, and they have a right to be there. "A faction," Publius said, "is a number of citizens, whether amounting to a majority or minority, of the whole, who are united and actuated by some common impulse of passion, or of interest, adverse to the rights of other citizens, or to the permanent and aggregate interests of the community."

Ambition must be made to counteract ambition, as the *Federalist* papers noted, and it is through this tenet embodied in the federal government that common interests can evolve. As Hamilton wrote, "In the extended republic of the United States, and among the great variety of interests, parties, and sects which it embraces, a coalition of a majority of the whole society could seldom take place on any other principles than those of justice and the common good." Before the end of Henry Clay's life, those principles would be sorely tested.

When Clay was a young man, the American republic was not capable of quickly assembling a Congress that could protect all our citizens against the designs of foreign powers. Since 1803, through two presidential administrations, America was little more than a guinea pig for the foreign policy aspirations of European nations. The Continent viewed America as a bootstrap country that had fought once for its independence but probably would not fight again. Contemporary British naval theorists were quick to point out the young country's current naval contingent of sixteen frigates was not a match for the battle-tested English navy of more than five hundred warships.

With such naval superiority, Great Britain proceeded to taunt the new republic. The English navy seized merchant ships and impressed their crews into involuntary service aboard British vessels and violated tariff agreements. After countless insults and failed negotiations, the American republic was finally able to populate Congress with legislators who were committed to using force to protect their nation's interests. In 1811, Capitol Hill welcomed the large freshman class of the Twelfth Congress. They were called War Hawks, and their leader was to be Henry Clay. Before the close of his first day in the House of Representatives, he was catapulted to the position of Speaker of the House and from that perch was better able to implement the War Hawks' agenda. They called for westward expansion for the new nation and military action against Great Britain. Clay forcefully called for an end to eight years of British antagonism against America.

Initially lacking national resources, Clay appeared powerless to achieve his goals. Our young country had no standing army and was less prepared than ever to stand toe to toe with a European power. Henry Clay had the role of an unarmed leader. He had to raise an army that almost simultaneously would be required to take the field. If the United States failed to produce a credible military force, it would be as if the country had actually fought a battle and lost. Some people speculated about whether America had achieved independence prematurely. What was needed more than the passion for liberty, which had buttressed the nation for the Revolutionary War, was a country capable of agreeing on a single-mindedness of purpose, united for the common good.

Henry Clay knew that if his country was to survive, grow, and reach its full potential in the world community, it would have to stand against breathtaking odds. Under the guidance of Clay, the Twelfth Congress passed a resolution trying to raise an army of twenty-five thousand troops for the sole purpose of winning the impending conflict with Great Britain. The unresolvable differences soon exploded into the War of 1812. Testifying to the mood of the times, only fifteen thousand troops were raised. Instead of a definitive American victory, we settled our dispute with Britain at the Treaty of Ghent, where Clay played an active and important role.

While seemingly a standoff, the war proved to be a de facto win for America. The country stood against a more powerful aggressor and emerged with its sovereignty intact. Clay confidently announced in a speech celebrating the treaty that "the effects of the war are highly satisfactory. Abroad, our character, which at the time of its declaration was in the lowest state of degradation, is raised to the highest point of elevation. It is impossible for any American to visit Europe without being sensitive to this agreeable change, in the personal attentions he receives, in the praises which are bestowed on our past exertions, and the predictions which are made as to our future prospects." The unexpected glory bestowed on America rescued the country from the envious eyes of other colonizing European powers and allowed the fledgling nation to extend its borders westward and settle the plains states with thousands of eager pioneers.

The momentary elevation was not an end in itself. Henry Clay saw it as merely a part of the whole. The unnerving delays in responding to the catalytic actions of the War of 1812 demonstrated that America did not yet have the extensive resources to quickly defend its interests. There was not a wide scope of interests to ensure an efficient republic in times of national stress, nor was it reasonable to assume that America would have had the endurance, or the power, to weather a union of its adversaries. There did not exist on the part of the people a commitment to ensure they would act together in matters of justice and the common good.

After the war, Clay sought to correct the deficit in the national will. During his twenty-seven years as an elected member of Congress, he developed what was later called the American system. It was not founded in ideology, but it was a material and commercial manifestation of the union between the states. Clay's system supported a national bank, federal aid to build roads and canals, and railroads to link the mushrooming republic's increasingly distant borders. To further this system, he participated in the westward growth of America and was a steadying and welcome influence through many political crises.

Though already proven to be an untiring servant before his retirement in 1842, Clay willingly left the pleasures of private life to author the Compromise of 1850. The need for the Compromise arose over the issue of slavery. Slave states felt threatened from

143

the increasing number of nonslave states. The admission of the territories of California, New Mexico, and Utah to the Union as free states would upset the political equilibrium of fifteen slave states to fifteen free states. Adding to the problem, free states opposed admission of any slave states. The air filled with talk of secession as Henry Clay introduced the Compromise of 1850 on the Senate floor.

As its author, Clay would receive the dubious nickname of "the Great Compromiser," a name some thought implied a lack of consistent principles. But Clay's handiwork needs no apology. He helped pull our nation away from the edge of disaster and delayed the start of war. The final bill provided that California be admitted to the Union as a free state, Texas a slave state, and ceded to New Mexico a portion of the land that Texas and New Mexico mutually claimed while $10 million in retribution was paid by the federal government. The District of Columbia abolished the slave trade but not slavery. The territories of New Mexico and Utah would determine their own positions on slavery when they petitioned for statehood. A new code, aimed at deterring escaping slaves, made it a criminal activity to help a fleeing slave.

After heated debate, the Compromise was accepted. Though it did not settle the issue of slavery, it allowed the republic another ten years before rifle and cannon would decide the issue forever. Henry Clay was against slavery, and we cannot assume that he believed its malignant effects could be cured by the Compromise. By initiating it, he was exercising the same political prudence demonstrated years before as leader of the War Hawks.

The Compromise of 1850 expanded the multitude of interests that governed our country. From coast to coast the special interests grew so diverse that the only common ground they could have was justice and the common good. The republic, as envisioned by the Founding Fathers and furthered by Henry Clay, was a nation whose geography, people, and institutions formed an indissoluble bond and had the power to address any tendency toward tyranny. A concerted republic allows for human desires to be governed and guided by a providential hand, yielding only what is good.

Had Henry Clay not been a dutiful servant to his God and his country, Abraham Lincoln might never have stood on the east steps of the Capitol and delivered two inaugural addresses. At least in part, Lincoln had Clay to thank for the opportunity to stand on those steps and profess his belief that the Civil War was America's atonement for the sins of slavery. We are forced to wonder, If a British soldier had not thrust his sword into the grave of Henry Clay's father, would the young Clay have led a life so galvanized toward the glory of liberty and freedom?

Clay's rhetorical skills mesmerized audiences with their force and logic. He once apologized for tiring after captivating the Senate gallery with a three-day speech. His sheer willpower and endurance made him a natural leader. While historians are sometimes distracted by his failed presidential campaigns, it is more instructive to review the man's fifty-year career in the federal government. No other member of the House has been so respected by his peers that he was elected Speaker in his first term in Congress or ran for president as the candidate for two political parties.

Those of us in public life would do well to follow Clay's example of hard work, reflection, and unfaltering insistence to pursue the public good. Today we hear much talk of the courage required to balance the federal budget or tackle emotional issues such as welfare reform. If Henry Clay could speak to us today, I believe he would point to the War of 1812 or the debate over slavery that tore our nation apart, and puzzle over why so many of today's leaders have so little faith in the ability of ordinary men and women to be responsible citizens.

Nearly one hundred fifty years after his death, Henry Clay's mark is still visible in the marble hallways of Congress and the gentle hills of his Kentucky home, and it is embodied in a nation that remains the shining beacon of liberty to oppressed peoples throughout the world.

Note: My special thanks to Joseph A. Monaghan, who assisted with the preparation of this article.

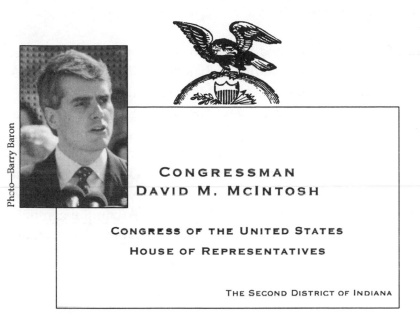

CONGRESSMAN
DAVID M. MCINTOSH

CONGRESS OF THE UNITED STATES
HOUSE OF REPRESENTATIVES

THE SECOND DISTRICT OF INDIANA

Raised in the farming town of Kendallville, Indiana, McIntosh graduated from East Noble High School, then paid his way through college by working at the Kendallville Foundry. He graduated from Yale College in 1980, having studied under future Supreme Court Justice Antonin Scalia. McIntosh received his law degree from the University of Chicago in 1983. He is a member of the bar of the United States Supreme Court and the state of Indiana.

Congressman McIntosh served as special assistant for Domestic Affairs under President Reagan and as special assistant to Attorney General Ed Meese, specializing in constitutional law. He also served as special assistant to Vice President Quayle and as executive director of the President's Council on Competitiveness.

A former Fellow at the Hudson Institute Competitiveness Center, chaired by Dan Quayle, McIntosh served as a Senior Fellow at Citizens for a Sound Economy. He founded the Federalist Society for Law and Public Policy and now serves as the conservative group's national cochairman.

Representative McIntosh and his wife, Ruthie, live in Muncie, Indiana. Ruthie served as staff director of First Lady Barbara Bush's Foundation for Family Literacy and as associate director of development at Ball State University.

Congressman McIntosh serves on the Government Reform and Oversight Committee and chairs its National Economic Growth, National Resources, and Regulatory Affairs Subcommittee. He also serves on the Economic and Educational Opportunities Committee.

How to Contact

> 1208 Longworth House Office Building,
> Washington, D.C. 20515
> Telephone: 202-225-3021
> Fax: 202-225-3382

☆ ☆ ☆ ☆ ☆ ☆ ☆ ☆ ☆ ☆ ☆ ☆ ☆ ☆

DAN QUAYLE WAS RIGHT! After decades of public dispute about so-called family diversity, the evidence from social-science research is coming in. The dissolution of two-parent families, though it may benefit the adults involved, is harmful to many children, and dramatically undermines our society.

—*Atlantic Monthly*, April 1993

L ike most of my freshman colleagues in the House of Representatives class of '94, I campaigned on themes that have long been identified with Dan Quayle. We believed that in November 1994, America stood at a critical crossroads. Voters resoundingly rejected the decades-old path of big government liberalism that has undermined the moral foundation of our great country, and they chose a path of freedom and the family. The people have called on their new generation of leaders to reduce the size and scope of a bloated federal government, expand individual freedoms, strengthen the American family as the centerpiece of our communities, and restore integrity and moral values to public service.

This is the Dan Quayle agenda. Even if I didn't agree with him on policy, Dan Quayle would be a leader I greatly admire because he has always demonstrated the courage of his convictions. Throughout his career, one thing has always been true of Dan Quayle; however difficult the battle, whatever the nature of the opposition, however highly charged the political environment, and whatever the odds of success, he has stood firm in his commitment to fundamental principles. He offers every person in public life, and every American, an example of steadfastness that is worth emulating. As President Nixon reminded us, Dan Quayle has been through fire and emerged with his pride and good humor intact, and his love for America undimmed.

Having worked closely with him, I know that his public and

private lives give eloquent testimony to the bedrock virtues that will take a person far in this modern world. My wife, Ruthie, and I seek to emulate virtues such as sticking to your principles and fighting, alone if you must, to defend them, staying in the battle for the long haul, and placing your trust completely in God and family. Possessing these qualities does not mean you will never lose a battle; it does mean you will not be a failure.

I first met Dan Quayle when I was in high school during his first campaign for Congress in 1976. He came to my hometown and urged us to become personally involved in the action and passion of politics. "You can make a difference, and you should try," he coaxed us. At twenty-nine, Quayle was already doing exactly that by giving an eight-term incumbent the race of his life and beating him on election day, despite a national Democratic Party trend. Four years later, against the odds and advice of virtually every political expert, he ran for the United States Senate and defeated another incumbent—the eighteen-year veteran, Senator Birch Bayh, Jr.

When my friends advised me not to run for Congress in 1994, I often thought of Dan's experience. Many said that I had two chances of winning: slim and none at all. But Ruthie and I persevered against the odds. We were firmly convinced it was time for individuals who believed in family values, lower taxes, less government, and more individual freedoms to be heard in Congress. Our uphill battle was blessed with the work of thousands of volunteers who believed in our message and totally supported us.

Who could have guessed that the incumbent, Phil Sharp, would retire and the leading Republican opponent would withdraw from the race? Even so, it was still a close primary, and I won by only 458 votes. I faced one of the leading Democratic candidates who also happened to be the sitting secretary of state. Throughout the race, I thought of Dan Quayle's two long-shot wins, and I believed that victory was possible. I also remembered Dan's advice: just tell people what you stand for and how you would represent them in Washington. Ruthie and I set that as our goal and decided that whatever the outcome on election day, we would judge our campaign a success if we could look ourselves in the mirror the day after the election and be proud of all we had done.

After the election in 1994, I sought Dan Quayle's advice on how to become an effective leader in Congress. Those of us who know Dan also know of his very successful career in the Senate. His accomplishments and well-tuned political skills caught the attention of George Bush, who as Republican presidential nominee in 1988 chose Quayle as his running mate. The national press corps took a very different view of him, however. Many political analysts now consider the days and weeks that followed Quayle's nomination for vice president to be the worst media feeding frenzy in modern times. Fueled by attack advertising from the campaign of Democratic nominee Michael Dukakis, as ABC News anchorman Peter Jennings later pointed out, the media's "pursuit of Quayle was relentless, and our demeanor was terrible."

As I watched the liberal media and Democratic campaign gurus hurl one false and misleading claim after another, I wondered whether Dan ever wished he could go back to being just plain Senator Dan Quayle, a hero to the folks back home in Indiana. Yet, the answer was very clear. Through it all, he soldiered forward to defend his convictions. His family, his friends, and Dan himself have told me it was the roughest period of his life. Only his deep faith in God and the sturdy love of the people who knew him best enabled him to persevere. Stand firm, they told him, we believe in you! You stand for principles that are stronger and more enduring than anything the opposition can throw at you.

Despite the ordeals of the campaign, the Bush/Quayle combination won a forty-state electoral landslide, and Dan Quayle was sworn in as vice president of the United States on January 20, 1989. It was an honor to join his staff as deputy legal counsel. About a year later, he assigned me to oversee the President's Council on Competitiveness. The group was formed to be the watchdog over the worst regulatory impulses of an arrogant and unaccountable federal bureaucracy. Thus began one of the most exciting chapters of my life, and the chance to view Dan Quayle's tenacity and determination at close range.

One of the Competitiveness Council's greatest struggles involved the protection of private property rights. During the 1988 campaign, George Bush had pledged that as president he would allow "no net loss" of wetlands in the United States. After he took office, a handful of career bureaucrats in the Environmental Protection Agency (EPA) used the campaign pledge as a pretext to secretly rewrite federal guidelines and covertly extend government power over private lives. They did that by expanding the definition of the term *wetland*. The immediate practical result was that huge tracts of dry land, including farms and even some desert areas, were designated as wetlands and fell under federal government control.

At the Competitiveness Council, I started to receive letters from families who were threatened with criminal charges if they so much as built an addition to the home. One letter came on behalf of a Polish-American immigrant. Mr. Polsby was actually arrested and jailed because he dared to fill in some abandoned land next to his family business. The episode left him wondering whether America was any better than the communist dictatorship that controlled his former homeland in Eastern Europe. The Polsby experience was a perfect illustration of the kind of bureaucratic arrogance, insensitivity, and government overreaching that the Council on Competitiveness was formed to combat. Though word had reached us too late to reverse the EPA decision on Mr. Polsby, I resolved right there and then that I would fight to put an end to the senseless and unfair restriction on private property.

Meanwhile, other government-induced regulatory horror stories were making their way to the vice president. During one of Quayle's frequent visits to the Midwest, a farmer told him, "Forget about all the other complaints we have about the federal government. The biggest enemy of farmers today is that wetlands crusade." The vice president called me into his office and directed me to make a wetlands policy the Council's top priority.

The staff at the Council dived straight into the issue and soon learned that things were worse than we had imagined. As Quayle later wrote in his vice presidential memoir, *Standing Firm*, "I was astonished to discover that thousands of acres of Indiana farm-land that I'd seen with my own eyes and walked over with my own dry feet were, by the EPA's standards, wetlands." After the vice president ordered us to oppose the new guidelines, some people advised him against taking overt action because it could hurt him politically.

He was cautioned that liberal environmental groups would undoubtedly charge that we were trying to break the president's pledge of "no net loss" of wetlands. Democratic Party congress-men hostile to the Council would step up their attacks, calling us everything from "an illegal shadow government" to a "polluter's star chamber." The vice president was told his detractors would try to besmirch the strong environmental track record he had already built in the House and Senate. Though I do not remember Quayle's exact words in response to these serious warnings, it was something along the lines of "we'll have to take that risk; it's the right thing to do."

Quayle was opposed to the new EPA manual. It trampled on basic American freedoms, and it had to go. We would continue to protect true wetlands that were important for the protection of environmentally sensitive ecosystems, but we would put an end to "wetland" regulations that prevented people from using their own dry land. The political pundits were correct; they accurately foretold that radical environmental groups would attack us. I remember watching one ad in particular on national television. It falsely accused us of forcing children to drink dirty water because we were rolling back wetlands protection. I began to wonder whether our reforms on behalf of small farmers and home owners, who couldn't afford to spend millions of dollars on TV ads, would survive the assaults.

A few presidential advisers were looking for ways to convince President Bush to dump Dan Quayle from the Republican ticket in 1992. The last thing I wanted was to have the Competitiveness Council wetlands reform issue used by them as evidence to the president that Quayle was not the right person to be his running mate. I'll never forget checking in with the vice president and asking, "Do you still want us to keep pushing to correct the wetlands abuses?" With a smile and a nod of his head, he reaffirmed us by simply saying, "Keep going." It was the right thing to do, and that was enough for him.

Ultimately, with the support of farmers, home owners, and property owners across the country, we were able to stop the EPA program in its tracks. Our victory, unfortunately, was temporary. Congress eventually intervened and forced us to compromise with the EPA. Nonetheless, it was heartening to see that the final draft did far less harm to private property rights than was the EPA's original intent.

There were a lot of other battles. The Council won just enough of them to make itself the number one enemy of a long list of proregulation special interest groups. As had become typical when Dan Quayle was involved, criticisms of the Council often degenerated into purely personal diatribes against the vice president. The *Wall Street Journal* wryly editorialized, "It wasn't long ago that Vice President Dan Quayle was said to be Washington's village idiot. All of a sudden he's becoming its scheming Rasputin. This can only mean he's begun to accomplish something." In my view, the editorialist could have added a warning to the special interest groups, "When you're in a fight with Dan Quayle over principle, don't expect ever to hear the word *surrender*."

Perhaps even more than his efforts to preserve individual freedoms, Quayle is best known for standing up for family values. Two words explain why his position on the sanctity of the family is so well known; they are *Murphy Brown*. Now often referred to as his famous Murphy Brown speech, delivered only three weeks after major riots in south-central Los Angeles, it was the defining moment of Quayle's vice presidency and sparked a national debate that continues to this day.

In that speech, Quayle's assertions about the breakdown of families and its terrible consequences to our society went largely ignored in favor of the more headline-grabbing comment that referred to an episode on the television show *Murphy Brown*. Quayle stated, "The lawless social anarchy which we saw [in the riots] is directly related to the breakdown of family structure, personal responsibility and social order in too many areas of our society." Unless we restored those values and eliminated a welfare system that had created a culture of dependency, Quayle warned, "Any attempt to fix what's broken will fail . . . , we will simply get more of what we saw three weeks ago." He called for a serious rethinking of the federal government's approach to antipoverty programs and asked the American people to enter into a national conversation on the values of family, integrity, and personal responsibility.

Of course, what was really the headline maker was the vice president's challenge to the popular culture. While other politicians had spoken about what Dan called the "poverty of values," Quayle was the first to point out publicly that basic moral values were being undermined by wider cultural influences. He emphatically pointed out that "it doesn't help matters when prime time TV has Murphy Brown—a character who supposedly epitomizes today's intelligent, highly paid, professional woman—mocking the importance of fathers by bearing a child alone, and calling it just another 'lifestyle choice.'" Contrary to the message espoused by the entertainment elite, Quayle explained that "all lifestyle choices are not created equal, and Americans should not be embarrassed out of their belief that two parents, married to each other, are better in most cases for children than one."

Hollywood and the press reacted quickly and angrily. The annual Emmy Awards program that year became a drawn-out attack on the vice president. The *Murphy Brown* scriptwriters had a field day. The news media that had never let go of the caricature they had created loosed a new barrage of negative stories on Quayle. No surprises there.

Even in retrospect, what is truly astonishing is that neither the White House nor the Bush reelection campaign people were willing to come to the vice president's defense. Presidential Press Secretary Marlin Fitzwater, who had initially spoken out in support of Quayle, began furiously backpedaling after only a few hours. The White House chief of staff told the vice president flatly, "This thing's a loser." As the controversy swirled around him, Quayle stood virtually alone. His response? Still in California the day after the speech, he stepped off *Air Force Two* and told a throng of agitated reporters that he "wouldn't change a single word." It was his finest hour.

If you have read subsequent reports about the fallout of this exaggerated incident, you know that Dan Quayle has been vindicated. Three months after he and President Bush left office, the

Atlantic Monthly, hardly considered a conservative screed, ran a cover story entitled "Dan Quayle Was Right." Barbara Dafoe Whitehead detailed the statistical evidence proving the disastrous consequences of family breakdown. Later, President Bill Clinton, whose first public reaction to the speech had been to attack Dan Quayle in harsh personal terms, told Tom Brokaw in one of his rare moments of candor, "I read [Dan Quayle's] whole speech, his Murphy Brown speech. I thought there were a lot of very good things in that speech." True to his character, the former vice president resisted the temptation to respond with a hearty "I told you so!"

Dan Quayle will forever represent family values in the political sphere, but the virtue of devotion to family is far more than an abstraction to him. The whole time I have known Marilyn and Dan Quayle, they have been deeply devoted parents to their three children. His wife is a full and invaluable partner in every decision Dan makes. As even the *Washington Post* has pointed out, "Family comes first for the Quayles, not just rhetorically in the speeches they both give, but in the ordering of their daily lives."

During his years in Congress, Dan Quayle was virtually invisible in the Washington social scene. He was home with his family. You always had the sense that if Dan's political life posed any threat to their family's happiness, the Quayles would give up politics in a heartbeat. Senator Bob Dole loves to tell the story about the day he received a letter from Senator Quayle's nine-year-old daughter, Corinne, telling of her upcoming appearance in a school play. She pleaded with Dole to "make sure there aren't any votes between 7:00 P.M. and 9:00 P.M., so my daddy can watch me." Senator Dole read the letter on the Senate floor, and Corinne got her wish.

If I had one concern that made me reluctant to enter elective politics, it was the prospect of what might happen to my family life. Ruthie and I were engaged during the 1992 campaign. It was a bright spot to look forward to as we both faced a mandatory career change after the elections. As we moved back to Indiana and pondered the pros and cons of running for Congress, the Quayles' example more than anything else helped resolve our concerns. Ruthie and I knew what to do. We must put each other, and our family, first in our lives. That meant every endeavor, whether it be campaigning, working, or making decisions, must be a joint effort. If political ambitions ever collided with family priorities, the family must win.

During our own campaign for Congress, Ruthie and I would say a quiet prayer asking God not to bring victory, but that we run the race in a way that stood for principle and in a manner that would reflect His will.

Ruthie likes to repeat the words of a song that states, "You've got to stand for something or you'll fall for anything." Dan Quayle has always stood for something, and he has shown uncommon courage in defending his beliefs. When blows from the media and opponents rained down on him, never once did he yield to the temptation to take pity on himself or look for the easy way out. Quayle once defined his spirit of resolve by writing, "With all my being, I have tried to stand firm, without wavering, for what I believe."

He has succeeded in this commitment, and his example speaks to all of us, regardless of the path we may choose for our own lives. Standing firm for your principles won't always win you friends or, for that matter, elections. It will, however, guarantee invisible rewards to which every one of us should aspire. Among them are self-respect, a clear conscience, and the satisfaction of knowing that you have made a difference.

Dan Quayle, perhaps better than many of his contemporaries, knows those hidden rewards. When the day comes for each of us to battle for what we believe is right, let us do it Dan Quayle's way. Thanking God for giving us an abiding faith that guides us, family and friends to encourage us, and a chance to carry the banner for a just cause.

CONGRESSWOMAN
SUE MYRICK

CONGRESS OF THE UNITED STATES
HOUSE OF REPRESENTATIVES

THE NINTH DISTRICT OF NORTH CAROLINA

Representative Myrick has an impressive record of business, civic, and political accomplishments. She first gained national attention through her work as a two-term (1987–91) mayor of Charlotte, North Carolina. As mayor, she was appointed to President Bush's Affordable Housing Commission, and she represented the National Conference of Mayors' Commission on Crime and Drugs.

Upon her election to the U.S. House of Representatives in 1994, Myrick was named one of the members of the House transition team responsible for ushering in the first Republican majority in forty years. Due in part to her solid performance on the transition team, Myrick was later drafted by her peers as a freshman liaison to the Republican leadership. In this capacity, she meets on a regular basis with the Speaker, majority leader, and other key members in carrying out the people's business.

Myrick brings a unique blend of business and personal experience to the nation's capital. She is the former president and CEO of Myrick Advertising, and she is a mother of five and a grand-mother of seven.

Myrick handily won her district seat in the 1994 general election with 65 percent of the vote. Her district is comprised of parts of Mecklenburg, Gaston, and Cleveland Counties, which are located in south-central North Carolina. She serves on the Budget, Science, and Small Business Committees and three sub-committees.

How to Contact

509 Cannon House Office Building,
Washington, D.C. 20515
Telephone: 202-225-1976
Fax: 202-225-3389

☆ ☆ ☆ ☆ ☆ ☆ ☆ ☆ ☆ ☆ ☆ ☆ ☆

I magine you are approaching the front door of an office building where you have an important appointment, and you cannot get inside. The door is not locked, but you can't reach it because you are in a wheelchair.

When I first learned of my opportunity to submit a chapter for this book, I immediately wanted to encapsulate the life of an extraordinary woman, Deborah Crouch McKeithan. The daughter of a Baptist preacher, Deborah has personal determination and quiet optimism that have touched the lives of hundreds, if not thousands, of Americans with disabilities.

Although she has multiple disabilities including legal blindness, cerebral multiple sclerosis, and epilepsy, Deborah has been working since 1979 to help other disabled Americans achieve their fullest potential and give effective and meaningful contributions to society. As founder and past president of Learning How, Incorporated, Deborah has garnered national attention for her efforts to establish a coast-to-coast support network for disabled people that meets their individual needs for a fuller life, professionally and personally. Her remarkable life has been the focus of well-known publications such as *Newsweek, New York Times, Family Circle,* and *Ms.* Taking her story to the airwaves, Deborah has been a guest on national radio talk shows and television programs including *Hour Magazine, CBS Morning News,* and *The Sally Jessy Raphael Show.*

As I spoke with Deborah recently, I was reminded of the level of daily commitment needed by a disabled individual to function in today's society, let alone succeed. Deborah's voice was frail. She had just returned home from the hospital after experiencing a seizure, an unfortunate but not uncommon occurrence in Deborah's life. In profiling Deborah McKeithan, I can only hope that these words will amplify her extraordinary story and inspire others as it has inspired me.

Deborah's childhood had little in common with most children. She was born with the virus of cerebral multiple sclerosis, and her early years were marked by tremors, poor vision, memory lapses, and a weakened immune system. Insensitive to her physical weaknesses, as youngsters often are, Deborah's classmates frequently mocked her maladies. Deborah's parents took her from doctor to doctor, but in those early years no diagnosis of her condition was forthcoming. After being struck by a car as a child, Deborah began to have seizures on a fairly regular basis. As she became older, the seizures became life-threatening.

At nineteen years of age, soon after graduation from high school, Deborah had a near fatal seizure that left her temporarily blind and paralyzed, and she lost her ability to hear or speak. After six months of hospitalization Deborah emerged with a desire to enter the nursing profession and devote her energies to helping others with physical disabilities. As one who knew more deeply than most just what it meant to have a serious disability, Deborah felt she was uniquely qualified to show empathy and understanding toward the needs of patients.

Unfortunately, as she neared completion of her nursing school training, Deborah had a terrible headache one night. After she checked herself into the hospital, her symptoms were misdiagnosed, and she was placed in the psychiatric unit. One day later she experienced a near fatal stroke that left her body paralyzed and unable to speak. Only then was Deborah officially diagnosed with cerebral multiple sclerosis.

During her hospitalization, Deborah and her family began to look for organizations that could help the family cope with her disability and its daily challenges. After leaving the hospital and spending months in rehabilitation, Deborah regained her ability to speak. She decided to do something that would forever change the focus of her life, although she was unaware of it at the time. She entered the North Carolina Miss Wheelchair Pageant. It was an experience that allowed her to meaningfully interact with other physically disabled women for the first time, and Deborah knew it was to play an important role in her life.

As Deborah explained, the pageant allowed her to bond with others sharing a similar situation. Deborah forged relations with several participants and found it was easier to talk freely to individuals with whom she could relate. After finishing as first runner-up and winning Miss Congeniality, she knew her new friendships would last. Shortly after that, Deborah and a group of women she met at the pageant decided to formally launch a support organization for other women who use wheelchairs.

The new organization's goals were to offer guidance and encouragement in the daily lives of women with disabilities. From their first meeting, held literally at a dining room table, was born the charter group for the Handicapped Organized Women, or HOW. This organization now encompasses more than one hundred chapters in thirty-nine states throughout our nation. As the founders of HOW, Deborah and her colleagues selected a few key organizational principles. One of the tenets is to allow any HOW member five minutes to tell others what she could not do because of her disability. This self-expression is allowed on one condition; the member must subsequently talk for five hours to tell others what she is willing to learn despite her disabilities!

This can-do philosophy is epitomized by Deborah's belief that HOW members should be "striving to be more and do more," and "to always be one step beyond the last step taken." In Deborah's words, HOW offered a new challenge for both disabled persons and their traditional caregivers. The driving force behind HOW's early success was its emphasis on service projects. Advocacy groups for disabled people have been the customary recipients of community service projects, but with HOW the group itself was assuming the role of community servant. Members of HOW would help themselves by first helping others.

An example of the fledgling group's early efforts was a North Carolina Christmas party hosted for refugee Vietnamese orphans. The little children who had never seen a Christmas tree or even a Christmas present had the time of their lives that night and not one of them noticed or cared or made mention that all of the hostesses used wheelchairs. The event taught the women that they, too, were needed in the world. The long-term result was that all HOW members must participate in two service projects a month to retain their membership.

From that Yuletide experience, word began spreading about the group's success, and before long other statewide chapters were formed. Just as the organization began to grow and blossom, Deborah had her first real bout with cerebral multiple sclerosis. For two long years, Deborah was usually hospitalized or confined to bed. During that period, Deborah turned to HOW for support and motivation. According to Deborah, "HOW had given me a true purpose in life." People with Deborah's disabilities need the support of others who fully understand what it means to cope with disabilities on a daily basis. As Deborah has stated, "When you see that much need, you've got to meet it."

Not satisfied with just performing service projects, Deborah used her position as HOW's leader to confront a serious political obstacle that stood before many physically disabled individuals. Faced with losing her health benefits if she took a job, Deborah wrote to then President George Bush requesting the Social Security disability laws be changed. Deborah wanted all people with disabilities to have the right to go back to work, earn what income they could, and purchase Medicare benefits depending on their earnings level.

Because of her insightful letter, Deborah was invited to testify before Congress, and she was named to the President's Committee on Employment of the Disabled. In those capacities, Deborah fought for the successful passage of the Disabled Americans

Work Incentive Act. Deborah was also a key influence in the passage of the Americans with Disabilities Act (ADA), which was made into law in 1990, and she has worked to provide equal access to facilities for more than forty million Americans with physical disabilities.

Deborah recently founded Learning How, Incorporated. It is an employment agency that specializes in placing physically disabled individuals in the workforce. Through her efforts, major employers now turn to Learning How when they need highly qualified and committed people. They have learned that physical disabilities do not impair the mind.

Deborah's story is a wonderful inspiration to me. She has an optimistic spirit that has opened avenues of personal freedom to millions of our citizens. Thanks to her selfless efforts in assuring passage of the Americans with Disabilities Act, discrimination against hiring workers with disabilities is no longer tolerated. Wheelchair ramps and accessible rest rooms and apartment facilities abound, and the rights of the persons with disabilities are no longer taken for granted.

In Deborah McKeithan, I am blessed to have a friend whose life epitomizes the ideals of optimism, determination, and persistence. In my daily walk I often reflect on Deborah, and I am encouraged by her successes. We cannot choose who we are in this world, when we would be born, or the physical attributes we will carry; but we can choose the mental attitude we will possess and the moral values we will hold dear as we live out our lives.

Deborah McKeithan's efforts on behalf of disabled persons have provided the courage for other disabled women to recognize that they, too, are needed in this world. Deborah and the tasks she has completed provide a stabilizing sense of peace and accomplishment in my life and in the lives of so many others who have personally benefited from her dedication to the rights of disabled persons. She truly deserves to be a profile in character.

Hard work and determination have marked the business, civic, and political activities of Congressman Neumann. Working his way through the University of Wisconsin-Whitewater by waiting tables and washing dishes, he graduated with honors in just three years.

In 1980, Neumann founded his own company, Milton Area Realty. He began Neumann Developments in 1986 to build houses. By 1991, he employed 250 people and was building 120 homes a year. The business earned national honors from *Inc.* magazine as one of the nation's fastest growing companies. In 1992, he sold the business, and a year later he launched Neumann Corporation, a real estate development firm.

Neumann was the 1994 recipient of the Entrepreneur of the Year award from the University of Wisconsin-Whitewater Entrepreneurship Program. He worked on Rock County's first Habitat for Humanity home. Neumann has been a member and officer of several civic and professional organizations and has shown special concern for young people. He has been a director of the Boys and Girls Club of Janesville and a volunteer basketball coach at the YMCA.

Neumann resides in Janesville with his wife, Sue, and their three children.

Neumann is a member of the House Appropriations Committee and the Budget Committee and several subcommittees.

How to Contact

1725 Longworth House Office Building,
Washington, D.C. 20515
Telephone: 202-225-3031
Fax: 202-225-3393

☆ ☆ ☆ ☆ ☆ ☆ ☆ ☆ ☆ ☆ ☆ ☆ ☆

In my business and government life I am frequently called upon to speak to a group and express my views on our nation's fiscal or social policy, usually whatever may be currently under consideration in Congress. Often, while enjoying dessert and waiting for the introduction that signals it is my turn to take the podium, I have noticed that most of the masters of ceremonies, narrators, or meeting leaders tend to follow a central theme.

Typically, they talk about my background in the home-building industry and the company that my wife and I created from nothing; it now builds more than 120 homes per year while providing employment for about 250 people. Sometimes they mention the awards we have received along the way, and they always mention my election to Congress. I am grateful that they do; after all, I may not be a household name to everyone in the audience. Of course, they never talk about the many failures endured along the road to success. Failures are potholes on the success highway.

I have experienced many defeats in my life. I remember losing an important basketball game while competing in a state tournament as an assistant coach. It is painfully easy to recall financial setbacks when our business was young, and the odds were fifty-fifty as to whether the business would even survive. Perhaps the most devastating defeat in my life came when I lost my second bid for a congressional seat. After weeks of reasonably positive campaigning, eleven days before the election my opponent discovered he was behind in the polls and switched his tactics to a negative advertising campaign. It included pictures of my family and derogatory comments about my abilities. Unfortunately, his negative attack ads worked.

After a recount in which 1,146 ballots were discarded, the officials decided that I had lost the race by 673 votes. At about the same time, a small fortune in campaign expense bills from unauthorized expenditures arrived. After surveying the wreckage, my family and I decided to stay in the private sector, and we started two new businesses. Both failed within six months.

Keeping failure in perspective is necessary if it is to be overcome. I have read and reread a passage from Scripture when things have not gone well, and it has helped me enormously in times of trial. James, the brother of Christ, wrote these edifying words:

> My brethren, count it all joy when you fall into various trials, knowing that the testing of your faith produces patience. But let patience have its perfect work, that you may be perfect and complete, lacking nothing. If any of you lacks wisdom, let him ask of God, who gives to all liberally and without reproach, and it will be given to him. But let him ask in faith, with no doubting, for he who doubts is like a wave of the sea driven and tossed by the wind. For let not that man suppose that he will receive anything from the Lord; he is a double-minded man, unstable in all his ways (James 1:2–8).

At times like these it is more than comforting to know that someone else has been in similar straits, burdened by loss after loss, and has rebounded to achieve success greater than he could ever imagine while depressed and disappointed. I know that history is replete with stories of men and women, the famous and not so famous, who found greatness after seemingly crushing events in their lives appeared to bring all their efforts to naught.

I have studied the life of such a man, the sixteenth president of the United States, Abraham Lincoln. Biographers and historians nearly always speak of the achievements of his political career. Not so well known is that before he became a great statesman, he experienced many failures in his personal and business lives. I am convinced that his reactions to frequent discouragement throughout his life molded the character capable of salvaging our nation from a terrible Civil War.

I would like to focus on Lincoln's failures because the many setbacks in business and politics and the tragedies in his personal life shaped the kind of man he became. The man he became shaped the presidency, and the presidency shaped our nation in its darkest days.

During the 1830s, Lincoln failed in a general merchandising business, he lost an election for the Illinois legislature, his future bride died from illness, he lost his attempt to become Speaker of the House in the state legislature, and he had a nervous breakdown from the stress of it all. In the words of one historian, "Some violent emotional disturbance did occur; indeed, no one can read Lincoln's correspondence from the period without being impressed with his excessive morbidity."

Those were just the more notable failures. Bankruptcy in business by itself would be enough to make a lesser man give up ambitious pursuits, but for Lincoln it was only the beginning of his problems. As he struggled to stand on his feet again after each defeat, he gained in maturity and inner strength.

A bright spot appeared in Abe's life in November 1842 when he married Mary Todd in a simple ceremony in Springfield, Illinois. She was at his side twenty-three years later in Ford's Theater in Washington, D.C. Lincoln was also the local postmaster and deputy county surveyor before winning election to the state legislature in 1834, and he held a variety of government posts before achieving national recognition. He served in the Illinois state legislature as a member of the Whig Party from 1834 to 1842, where he first spoke out against slavery. Lincoln served competently but without notoriety until 1854 when again as a Whig, his fiery speech against slavery brought him national acclaim. The speech was in response to the repeal of the Missouri Compromise of 1820, an act that brought the issue of slavery to the forefront of American politics.

When the Republican Party was organized in 1856, largely to

combat the extension of slavery, Lincoln left the Whig Party and became the Republicans' most prominent leader in Illinois. Delegates from his home state nominated him for the vice presidency. He lost the election to Stephen A. Douglas, one of the most able debaters of his day, and spent the next four years supporting the abolitionist cause. After the defeat Lincoln took a leadership position in the fledgling Republican Party, but it wasn't until the third ballot of the May 1860 nominating convention that he became the party's choice. Later that year, he won the popular vote and became America's sixteenth president.

Abraham Lincoln was first a highly principled man. His devotion to ending slavery was founded in his deep conviction that all people truly are created equal. Nowhere else in his writings and speeches is this more evident than in the message conveyed to us in his stirring Gettysburg Address. Delivered in November 1863 at the commemoration of a new national cemetery at the battlefield site of one of the deadliest battles of the Civil War, this short but emotionally powerful speech begins as a moving testimonial to those who died to save their country, and it ends in a final sentence that states the true purpose of a free government is to be responsible to its people. I would like to share with you this address:

> Four score and seven years ago our fathers brought forth on this continent, a new nation, conceived in liberty, and dedicated to the proposition that all men are created equal.
>
> Now we are engaged in a great civil war, testing whether that nation or any nation so conceived and so dedicated, can long endure. We are met on a great battlefield of that war. We have come to dedicate a portion of that field, as a final resting place for those who here gave their lives that that nation might live. It is altogether fitting and proper that we should do this.
>
> But in a larger sense, we cannot dedicate, we cannot consecrate, we cannot hallow this ground. The brave men, living and dead, who

struggled here, have consecrated it, far above our poor power to add or detract. The world will little note, nor long remember what we say here, but it can never forget what they did here. It is for us the living, rather, to be dedicated here to the unfinished work which they who fought here have thus far so nobly advanced. It is rather for us to be here dedicated to the great task remaining before us, that from these honored dead we take increased devotion to that cause for which they gave the last full measure of devotion; that we here highly resolve that these dead shall not have died in vain; that this nation, under God, shall have a new birth of freedom; and that government of the people, by the people, for the people, shall not perish from the earth.

The Gettysburg Address holds special meaning to me as I work with my freshman colleagues in the 104th Congress. To me, the language Lincoln used in the address illustrates that he was a pragmatist and did not perceive himself as the truly great president that our history has declared. As president, Lincoln was able to change America because he remained focused on the cause he deeply believed in all his life.

Only my faith in God and the loving support of my family, especially my wife, Sue, allowed me to come back from the series of defeats I experienced prior to my successful campaign for Congress. In 1993, after two losses in congressional races and two business failures in a span of eighteen months, I was so tired of feeling defeated that I could not have made the decision to start a third business without my family and my faith.

The third business succeeded! By June 1994, our business was again booming, and our lives had returned to normal. What a great country is this United States! Maybe good things really do run in threes, but for the third time in three years I chose to step aside from running a successful business and try to make a difference in the future of our nation. The high personal price I paid getting to that point makes it easier to stay focused and on track. Clearly, Lincoln also paid a great personal price in his endeavor to free the slaves and preserve the union. Perhaps knowing that made him grasp his beliefs even more strongly.

As we rapidly move through the 1990s, there are two issues of comparable importance to the slavery issue of Lincoln's generation. They are balancing the federal budget and the tremendously emotional issue of abortion. It has been so long since this nation has had a balanced federal budget that many are asking if it really matters anymore. The answer is, yes, it does. The financial mess in which we now find ourselves is not just a money problem; it is the reflection of the loss of moral values in our nation.

An entire generation has now lived with its hands in the pockets of our children and even our grandchildren. Members of my generation should be ashamed that they have spent $5 trillion of their children's money. This is immoral and unethical. What responsible parent would borrow money with the expectation that his or her children would pay it back?

The other lightning rod that will activate Americans to take up the banner against unethical behavior by our government may very well be abortion. Whatever America's policy on abortion may be, it is a statement to our citizens and the world about where we stand as a nation. An America that condones live-birth abortions when the life of the mother is not at risk should reconsider the entire foundation upon which all its moral values are based.

To paraphrase the Gettysburg Address, I believe that we are now engaged in a great social and economic civil war, and that Washington is the battlefield for that war. In a larger sense, we do not have the ability to repay the brave men, living and dead, who have struggled before us in these chambers to preserve this great nation. The world will neither little note nor long remember what we write here, but future generations will reap the results or suffer the consequences of what we accomplish here.

We must begin anew with a set of values worth fighting for

and be willing to keep rising from any defeat, fully committed to the core beliefs that first brought us to Congress.

CONGRESSMAN
CHARLIE NORWOOD

CONGRESS OF THE UNITED STATES
HOUSE OF REPRESENTATIVES

THE TENTH DISTRICT OF GEORGIA

This sprawling nineteen-county district in northeastern Georgia gave Norwood his first political victory with a resounding 65 percent of the vote. His pledges to fight for cuts in taxes and federal spending helped fuel his landslide victory.

A retired dentist, Norwood opposes federally mandated universal health coverage but supports changes in the current system. He is dedicated to finding a way to provide more affordable care without raising taxes.

Norwood favors legislation that combines stricter penalties for violent criminals with the requirement they serve their full sentences. He also favors increasing the number of police officers available to fight crime.

A native of Valdosta, Congressman Norwood lives in Evans, Georgia, with his wife, Gloria. They have two children.

Norwood's Tenth District includes Athens, home of the University of Georgia with more than 29,000 students, many of whom are voters; and Augusta, with a substantial population of military personnel from Fort Gordon. The Tenth District extends through rural cotton, soybean, and tobacco country.

Representative Norwood serves on the Commerce and Economic and Educational Opportunities Committees and three subcommittees.

How to Contact

> 1707 Longworth House Office Building,
> Washington, D.C. 20515
> Telephone: 202-225-4101
> Fax: 202-225-3397

☆ ☆ ☆ ☆ ☆ ☆ ☆ ☆ ☆ ☆ ☆ ☆ ☆ ☆

O ur nation's Capitol has a beauty that warms the spirit. At night, the splendor of lights on the mighty Capitol dome is enough to give you goose bumps. On a sunny day, you can look down from atop Capitol Hill and see the Smithsonian Institution, affectionately called our nation's attic, dispersed along the Mall. Looking farther, you see the majesty of the Washington Monument. In the distance, three and a half miles away, is the quiet grandeur of the seated Abraham Lincoln presiding over his memorial. If the day is particularly clear, your eyes will carry you beyond the Lincoln Memorial, over the Potomac River via Memorial Bridge, and through the wide gates of Arlington National Cemetery.

Arlington is one of the most moving symbols of what it means to be an American. Rows and rows of simple white crosses and headstones stand like miniature white-draped soldiers in perfect formation, marking the graves of men and women who gave their utmost to America, self-sacrificing so that millions of others might live their American dream. They displayed unbelievable courage in the face of insurmountable odds. Congressional Medal of Honor recipients lie alongside the lesser known, while the Tomb of the Unknowns touches the heart of all who witness its solemnity.

On a hill surveying the calm of Arlington is the historical home of Robert E. Lee, commanding general of Confederate forces during the American Civil War. As a southerner, I have always held General Lee in the highest regard. One reason is the choice he made to fight for Virginia. Lee led Virginia to war because he felt a compelling duty to his family and his ancestral home.

From all I have read about General Lee, I believe him to be a great patriot. He devoted most of his adult life to the United States Army. He fought in the Mexican-American War, and he led the army against the violent abolitionist, John Brown, at Harpers Ferry, Virginia. He was a soldier of distinction in the service of his country. I have never found anything that suggested Lee left the Union army to defend slavery for the South. Though he did not speak of it often, Lee was clearly troubled by slavery. He thought that human bondage contradicted all that was good and Christian, and that the eradication of slavery was inevitable. He rightly observed, "Is it not strange that the descendants of those pilgrim fathers who crossed the Atlantic to preserve their own freedom of opinion, have always proved themselves intolerant of the spiritual liberty of others."

In January 1861, Lee was deeply disturbed by the looming possibility of civil war. For him, the Civil War was about defending his home, his native state, and his honor. Shortly before war broke out, Lee wrote on this subject: "I wish to live under no other government, and there is no sacrifice I am not ready to make for the preservation of the Union, save that of honour. If a disruption takes place, I shall go back in sorrow to my people and share the miseries of my native state, and save in her defense, there will be one soldier less in the world than now."

The American Civil War began with the intensive shelling, followed by surrender, of Fort Sumter, a Union stronghold on a tiny island in the harbor of Charleston, South Carolina. Lee was quickly offered the command of a large federal army and a promotion to major general. His task would be to lead that army against the secessionists. Lee simply could not bring himself to launch a fighting force against his Southern contemporaries. He explained his painful refusal by saying, "I declined the offer . . . made [to] me to take command of the army that was to be brought into the field, . . . that though opposed to secession and deprecating war, I could take no part in an invasion of the Southern States."

For generations the Lee family had been Virginians and

Americans. Lee's forefathers had signed the Declaration of Independence, and his grandfather was a former governor of Virginia. In the final analysis, the Lees were Virginians before there was an America. For Robert E. Lee, difficult as it was, the only choice was to defend Virginia.

The personal price he paid for leading the Southern troops was extremely high. His fine home in Arlington was confiscated by federal troops and turned into a national cemetery, ensuring that Lee would never return to it. Personal friendships he had developed over many years with fellow officers in the Union army evaporated. He led the Army of Northern Virginia for four years, and even in defeat, with bloodshed and destruction of the South all about him, Lee never doubted his course. After the war, he spoke of the conviction of his decision: "I did only what my duty demanded. I could have taken no other course without dishonour. And if it were to be done over again, I should act precisely in the same manner."

It has been more than one hundred thirty years since the Civil War concluded. It remains as perhaps the most written about subject in our history. I know that for some, it is hard to separate the inherent evils of slavery from the honor and duty of defending one's home. Lee chose the defense of his home, family, and beliefs. I have always respected him for the courage of his choice.

I have walked among the headstones at Arlington and come upon a few that are for friends I knew in Vietnam. It was only by the grace of God that I did not join them where they now lay. As many generations before me, I went to war when called. For me in those times, it was a simple matter of duty to my country. World War II was a "popular" war. That is, the commitment of U.S. soldiers in defense of liberty had the total support of the American people.

The Vietnam War was not popular. Like the Civil War, it divided our nation sharply. There was tremendous public turmoil over Vietnam, but for me and many others in my generation, we went there in the midst of controversy because we believed it was right. It was our duty to our homes and families and the generations before us who fought in other unknown, seemingly unimportant places. It was the honorable thing to do.

In my view, dodging my patriotic responsibilities would have brought dishonor to me and my family. In 1967, I had a wife and two young children. The last thing I wanted to do was to go to war. I could have asked for a deferment, but I went to Vietnam anyway. Unlike General Lee's heart-tearing decision, mine was simpler. When your country calls, you go. I felt a personal responsibility connected to my deep belief in our free society. Our president and Congress are the duly elected leaders of our country. I believe these men and women strive to do their best and consider first what is good for America. I am firmly convinced that in time of war all citizens have a duty to follow their elected leaders.

Vietnam turned out to mean many things to me. It was sometimes exhilarating and sometimes terrifying. Was it character building? No, because I was already twenty-seven years old. I had been through dental school, and I had watched the birth of my two sons. By then, my character was well formed. Was I blindly brave in the face of great danger? To the contrary, I was scared silly much of the time. Others tell me this is a common feeling when people are shooting at you. I did what was asked of me to the best of my ability, regardless of the risk. When it meant going in harm's way to bring aid to a soldier in need, I felt it my duty to give all I could.

Twenty-five years later it seemed to me that our leaders were failing to see what was in America's best interests. I felt called by a different kind of duty to run for Congress. I entered the race because I was exasperated with the way the federal government affected my life, my family, and my community. I had a new duty to try to set things right. Running for Congress was just as scary—and more so in some ways—than going to Vietnam. I was gambling with my family's future, and those stakes were much greater than putting only myself in harm's way.

Of course, my fears were allayed when I won the congressional seat from the Tenth District of Georgia. I am worried that so many young people in America are growing up without any sense of duty. I fear that my grandchildren could find themselves in an America where individualism trumps any effort for the community good, where the rights of one outweigh the best interests of the whole, and where God is relegated to a distant figure who can't be part of the public forum. We are moving away from the core beliefs upon which our nation was founded.

So many ordinary things should be considered part of our duty to society. We must stay informed about issues in government that can change our lives. We have a responsibility to express our views, not only on the traditional soapbox, but through the ballot box. It is unthinkable to me that a good turnout is considered to be 50 percent of the eligible voters.

More Americans must embrace a fundamental and private duty. If you are able, you should work. I cannot for a moment imagine being able-bodied and not working. No American should ever view welfare as a viable lifestyle that replaces working. If you are physically and mentally able, you have a duty to contribute to the society in which you live.

If you father a child, you have a duty to see to that child's well-being. It is morally wrong that one-third of the children in America today are born out of wedlock. Fatherhood is a solemn duty. I have spent my adult life working to be a good father and adequate provider for my children. For me, that was the duty I accepted when my wife and I began our family. It is appalling to me that so many fathers have decided that taking responsibility for the new lives they have created is optional.

I look at the choice made by Robert E. Lee, to stay with the army in which he had served all his life, or leave it to defend his home. His decision to follow the duty of home and family must have been incredibly difficult, but he knew in his heart it was the right road for him. I sincerely hope the young people of America can find in their hearts a sense of duty to accomplish what is best for their families and communities.

We have a responsibility to our nation to be accountable for our actions. This country was founded on the discipline that government is responsible to us, not for us. There are no governmental guarantees of happiness, there is only the constitutional right to pursue it. These immortal words of President John F. Kennedy in his inaugural address—"Ask not what your country can do for you; ask what you can do for your country"—have not dimmed with the passing of time, and they pointedly show the way for Americans to find their duty.

We have established a unique form of government that allows us to remain free if we remember our duties to that freedom. The duty is to be responsible for ourselves and those in our charge, the duty to serve when called and the duty to defend our freedoms and our nation when challenged. If we do this, we shall pass to the next generation a stronger and better America.

I have now answered the call to duty twice in my lifetime, once in Vietnam and again in the Congress of the United States. Following your individual duty may not be easy, but as Lee said, "Duty is the sublimest word in our language. Do your duty in all things. You cannot do more. You should never do less." I hope that all my fellow citizens will choose to act honorably, seek God's will for their lives, and eagerly pursue their duty. Making this choice is the essence of being an American.

Note: The particular volume I have relied on for background and quotes in this essay is Richard Harwell's 1961 abridgment of the Pulitzer Prize–winning four-volume *R. E. Lee*, by Douglas Southall Freeman. It is a tremendous biography that I wholeheartedly recommend.

CONGRESSMAN
MATT SALMON

CONGRESS OF THE UNITED STATES
HOUSE OF REPRESENTATIVES

THE FIRST DISTRICT OF ARIZONA

Representative Salmon weathered a five-way contest in the 1994 Republican primary election to emerge as the candidate for the First District, which comprises most of Mesa, Tempe, and southeastern Phoenix. What makes his victory notable was that Salmon did not run a single ad in the primary campaign, but relied on a superior grassroots organization of door-to-door visits and direct mail. In what was expected to be a close race, Salmon defeated his Democratic opponent in the general election by seventeen points.

Salmon is not a political newcomer, having served with distinction in the Arizona senate from 1991 to 1995. In only four years, he became assistant majority leader and Rules Committee chairman. He worked in the Arizona legislature to pass legislation reforming the welfare system.

Salmon has a master's degree from Brigham Young University and is a former communications company executive. He resides in Mesa with his wife, the former Nancy Huish. They have four children.

Congressman Salmon serves on the International Relations, Science, and Small Business Committees and on six subcommittees.

How to Contact

115 Cannon House Office Building,
Washington, D.C. 20515
Telephone: 202-225-2635
Fax: 202-225-3405

☆ ☆ ☆ ☆ ☆ ☆ ☆ ☆ ☆ ☆ ☆ ☆ ☆ ☆

Throughout our brief history as a nation, Americans have always had a big place in our hearts for those who do heroic deeds. We love heroes, and we love to extol their virtues, whether a hero like Nathan Hale who regretted he had but one life to give for his country or the man who dived into the icy Potomac River and gave his life to save others. We even respect make-believe heroes such as Batman and Superman. We see a special something in a hero that we wish to emulate. The warm feeling that comes over us when we read of a heroic deed helps us overcome the cynical headlines from the morning paper, restores our faith in human beings, and gives us a smattering of hope.

A common contemporary theme played out in the media draws a distinction between a true hero and a person whose fame or notoriety is the result of excellence in a field of endeavor. Headlines in the paper are replete with references to athletes, actors or actresses, or popular music figures whose fine performances on the playing field, court, or stage are offset by private lives in shambles. They are either the victims or the volunteers for drug abuse, alcoholism, spousal abuse, frequent scrapes with the law, and multiple failed marriages.

Because of the dichotomy between real heroism and remarkable talent possessed by a few, I suggest it's time we take stock of America's moral heroes. It's time to focus on our country's unsung heroes, the men and women who silently march through their lives fulfilling their sense of duty and honor because they believe it is the right thing to do. The noblest heroes are those who in the face of adversity gave all they had and willfully put their very lives on the line when necessary.

They have known full well that their stories are unlikely to be told and their accomplishments unlikely to be celebrated. These men and women give of themselves freely, almost never complain about their lot in life, and possess a keen sense of personal responsibility. In total, these unrecognized heroes understand that true success in life is predicated on one's code of honor and behavior, and one's reactions to personal challenges.

I was fortunate to be raised by one of these unsung heroes. He is my father, Robert James Salmon. Understanding my father's life and the choices he made is like looking through a window in time and seeing how the character of an unsung hero is formed. Dad was born at Holy Cross Hospital in Salt Lake City, Utah, on October 1, 1923. He was the oldest of three boys born to Lorenzo S. Salmon and Helen Jane Hauerbach. When my father was six years old, during the earliest days of the Great Depression, Grandfather walked out on Grandmother and her tiny sons, never to return and never to provide one dime of support to his destitute family.

In today's society, my father would have been evaluated by a child welfare department of some sort and labeled an at-risk child. Undoubtedly, the family would have qualified for many overlapping government-subsidized welfare programs. In those days, before the welfare system, AFDC, and food stamps, families in a serious financial situation relied on their own devices and strength of character to make ends meet. Helen Salmon was a proud and independent woman who worked as a secretary to support her young family. When my dad was nine years old, he found his first job, operating a push mower at the local park. He worked all day for twenty-five cents, and that meager amount went to feed the family.

At fourteen, the age when today's kids are mastering video games, Dad secured a regular job as a butcher's apprentice in a small grocery store. He made all of seventeen cents an hour. One hour of his labor would buy about a dozen eggs in 1937. He would rise before 4:00 A.M. and work for two hours before going to school. When school was finished for the day, it was back to the butcher shop to work until midnight, four or five nights a week. He also contributed that money to the family treasury.

The summer after his graduation from high school he joined the Civilian Military Training Corps and earned an award as the most outstanding cadet. Because of his efforts, he was offered a scholarship to Hill Military Academy in Oregon, but he declined the offer. Instead he attended the University of Utah, where he studied anthropology and sociology for two quarters. Although Dad said he was fascinated by the prospect of "digging up old bones," he decided there wasn't much future in it and left the college scene. Despite limited finances, he enjoyed a very brief athletic career by playing for the university polo team.

In Southeast Asia, Dad went to work for the Ninth Service Command as a mechanic supplying the American forces, which at that time were involved in the war only on an unofficial basis. He continued that work until the Japanese forcibly brought the United States into World War II with their attack on Pearl Harbor in December 1941.

Although offered an essential civilian personnel deferral by the local draft board, Dad decided to enlist. Just before his enlistment in early 1942, he received his draft notice for the army. While he was home on final leave before being shipped overseas, his mother gave him a gift of a leather-bound, pocket-size copy of Rudyard Kipling's wonderful poem "If." With it was a copy of the New Testament. Dad said he frequently read both books during the long weeks and months of exhausting training and later in the oppressive jungles of New Guinea. Those cogent writings molded his thinking as he reflected on his favorite verses again and again.

Dad first reported for duty as a new army inductee at Fort Douglas near Salt Lake City. From there, he was transferred to Camp Roberts near Paso Robles, California, for rigorous basic training. Throughout his infantry indoctrination, the officers frequently noticed his outstanding mental abilities. He was offered a full scholarship to attend Stanford University to complete his education, then to return to the military as a commissioned officer. Later, he was offered the opportunity to attend the famous military school in South Carolina, the Citadel.

Because at that stage of his young life he preferred action to learning, he turned down both opportunities and was soon sent across the Pacific to join an infantry battalion in Finschhafen, New Guinea. The journey by ship lasted twenty-eight days. About three days out to sea, Dad was stricken with appendicitis. In a ship's operating room about the size of a closet, Lieutenant Worm performed his very first operation. My dad was the lucky patient! The night after his surgery Dad noticed that two other soldiers sat by his bed, holding a life jacket, for the entire evening. The next day they explained to my father that an enemy submarine had been detected in the ship's path and they were instructed to put the life jacket on him and toss him overboard if the ship was attacked. What a comforting bit of news to hear while recovering from surgery!

Upon arrival in New Guinea, Dad was assigned as his platoon's Browning automatic rifle (BAR) man. After noting that the rapid-firing BAR quickly marked its owner as a target for snipers, he modified the stock and sawed off its tripod in the hopes of maintaining a lower profile. Because of his obvious leadership capabilities, he received the rank of buck sergeant and the chance to attend Officer Candidate School in Brisbane, Australia. At the conclusion of training he would be commissioned a second lieutenant and sent to the Philippines. Owing at least in part to the fact that second lieutenant's bars also marked a soldier as a desirable sniper target, he concluded he would rather serve out the remainder of his career in relative anonymity at his new post in Biak, one of the Schouten Islands off the coast of New Guinea.

Three weeks before the Japanese surrender in 1945, Dad was

overcome by malaria and dengue fever, the seriousness of which resulted in his return to the U.S. The war having ended, he received his honorable discharge at Fort Douglas and once again became a civilian. After nearly a four-year absence, he found his mother had remarried, and his stepfather was the Salt Lake City dogcatcher. My mother has always reminded my siblings and me that we should refer to that particular position as a canine tax specialist. Like many veterans returning from the war, Dad found that there were many applicants for relatively few jobs, work was scarce, and pay was low. He did the best thing he could under the circumstances and became his stepfather's assistant.

During that time, he met and married a beautiful dark-eyed brunette, the former Gloria Bollette Aagard. When they married, Mom had three young children of her own: my oldest brother, Johnny, Steve in the middle, and my sister Dana, the baby. Mom and Dad had three additional children: Bob and Scott and me, the baby of the entire family.

I consider it one of the great tributes to my father that until I was eighteen years old, I never knew Dad was not the biological father of my three oldest siblings. In fact, none of us knew about our relationship with one another until we all learned of it together inadvertently. Withholding this important bit of information about the family tree may at first seem odd, but it explains Dad's loving concern that the family not be divided into two camps, with three children in each one. Although it required skillful omission of details on his part when I inquired about my parents' early lives, I later discovered my father never wanted any of his children to say in anger to one of the others, "He's not really your dad!" He knew how cruel children can be during their childhood and adolescent years. Even to this day, I could never think of my two older brothers and sister as half brothers and half sister. It just wouldn't be right.

One of the most poignant and touching moments of my young

life was when I saw my father cry for the first time. It happened when my brother Johnny died tragically in an auto accident near our home. During those awful days after Johnny's death and years later, when we would take out some personal memento that had been Johnny's, the tears would flow. Dad's grief was so genuine that I never doubted for a moment the depth of his love for my brother. I have always been certain that his love is every bit as great for each of his children.

I recall the time when my brother Steve badly needed a new winter coat. Winters are mighty cold in Salt Lake City. Finances were very tight and the money just couldn't be found anywhere in the family budget, but that didn't stop Bob Salmon. He sold his service revolver, a prized remembrance of his war years, and bought the coat for Steve. I know he never thought twice about it.

Having learned to operate Caterpillar tractors and Sherman tanks in the army turned out to be a valuable asset. Dad landed a job driving a big yellow Caterpillar with the Utah Construction Company. They were transforming Las Vegas from a small-town desert crossroads into the gambling mecca that now exists. Dad hated the long stretches of time apart from his new wife and family that the job required. Because he was fighting recurring bouts of malaria, he returned to Salt Lake City and was employed by the Mountain Bell Telephone & Telegraph Company.

According to Dad, he started at the top (the top of the ground, that is) as a posthole digger. He worked his way up through many of the trades available at Ma Bell, working as a construction lineman, maintenance lineman, and installer. Although eligible for military medical disability benefit payments, he was so busy working he hadn't enough time to keep up with the medical examinations required, and after eighteen months the payments stopped.

Dad typically worked three and sometimes four jobs during

the course of a week. He did it because none of them paid well enough for the life he hoped to provide for his family. During the brief span of one week, he was a night security guard every other night until 1:00 A.M. at Don Carlos Arctic Circle. Apparently, there were some really tough guys who wanted ice cream late at night. He worked at a drive-in movie theater until 12:00 or 1:00 A.M. two nights of the week. Weekends were not set aside for relaxation. Dad would work on Saturdays and Sundays building irrigation head gates at a local farm, scrub and wax floors in commercial stores, and labor with pick and shovel at the Murray Smelter in Murray, Utah.

It was a tough and exhausting lifestyle, and some days he would be so tired and sore, I knew it was a herculean effort just to get out of bed. One early morning, Dad was so tired when he got home from his security guard position that he accidentally shot a hole in the bedroom ceiling while unloading his revolver. On another occasion he broke the instep of his foot while operating a runaway jackhammer. The telephone company took a dim view of on-the-job accidents, so Dad didn't report the injury. He couldn't afford to lose that job, so he slept with his boot on for three weeks. He knew if he took the boot off he would never get it on again because of the painful swelling. He had a family to take care of, and he didn't take that job lightly.

This is the stuff that unsung heroes are made of. Never once did we children hear him complain. Not once did he ever ask us to do without, even though his shoes had holes in them and his clothes were worn long after their resemblance to a particular fashion style was gone. Without ever saying a word, but by his living example, he instilled in each member of my family a work ethic that demanded we give our best, asking only for an honest day's pay in return for an honest day's work. Without consciously thinking about it, he was our greatest teacher, and we students learned by observing.

Things went well with the phone company, and Dad was promoted to installer. His assignment on the first day of the new job was to remove old phones, and he removed twenty-five during his eight-hour shift. Back at the station the union steward took him aside and chastised his performance. It seemed that removing more than eight phones in an eight-hour shift made the other union members look bad. He told my dad to slow down if he knew what was good for him. Of course, Dad never compromised his work ethic by stopping at eight.

Bob Salmon earned his first promotion to a management position about ten years after digging his first posthole. He continued to climb the management ranks at Mountain Bell and achieved the rank of division network manager, what Bell called a fourth-level position. Dad accepted retirement at age sixty-two because he could not bear to see his beloved telephone company broken into numerous Baby Bells as dictated by a court decision.

Since it is possible that at some point my father is likely to read this, I should probably stop repeating his virtues in public. The Talmud wisely cautions, "Only a fraction of a man's virtues should be enumerated in his presence." I did not have the opportunity to know my grandmother, Helen Jane Hauerbach Salmon, who died before I was born. If I could speak to her today, I would surely tell her, "Thank you for the gift of your unselfish love, and for the words by Rudyard Kipling that helped mold my father's life."

If

*If you can keep your head when all about you are losing theirs
and blaming it on you;
If you can trust yourself when all men doubt you but make
allowance for their doubting, too;
If you can dream and not make dreams your master;
If you can think and not make thoughts your aim;*

If you can meet with triumph and disaster and treat those two
  impostors just the same;
If you can force your heart and nerve and sinew to serve your
  turn long after they are gone,
And so hold on when there is nothing in you except the will
  which says to them, hold on!
If you can fill the unforgiving minute with sixty seconds worth
  of distance run;
Yours is the earth and everything that's in it,
And which is more, you'll be a man, my son!

I proudly dedicate this writing to my personal unsung hero, my dad.

CONGRESSMAN
MARK SANFORD

CONGRESS OF THE UNITED STATES
HOUSE OF REPRESENTATIVES

THE FIRST DISTRICT OF SOUTH CAROLINA

Mark Sanford was born in 1960 and grew up on a family farm not far from Beaufort, South Carolina. On the farm, Sanford and his sister and two brothers learned that hard work and a quality education were essential for success. After attending high school in Beaufort, he graduated from Furman University in 1983 and the University of Virginia's Darden School of Business in 1988.

For the past decade, Sanford has worked in real estate finance and investment in New York and Charleston. Sanford and his wife, Jenny, live in Charleston with their three children. They attend St. Stephen's Episcopal Church.

Congressman Sanford's comprehensive business background earned him a position on the Joint Economic Committee, which is composed of members from both the House and the Senate. His commonsense approach to reforming the government gave him a seat on the Government Reform and Oversight Committee, as well as the International Relations Committee.

How to Contact

1223 Longworth House Office Building,
Washington, D.C. 20515
Telephone: 202-225-3176

☆ ☆ ☆ ☆ ☆ ☆ ☆ ☆ ☆ ☆ ☆ ☆ ☆

Many of our family treasures, the records of our heritage that reach back more than a hundred years, are stored in the attic of the barn on our family farm in South Carolina. It's an old barn, so the roof leaks, and some of these treasures are in danger of being ruined. Getting to that barn and sorting through the old and often weathered letters, photos, and documents had been on my "things to do" list for much too long. I wanted to save these things for our three children and, someday, our grandchildren.

With the hectic pace of my campaign and subsequent election to Congress, I did not have the time to undertake this task. Finally, during the recess of August 1995, I climbed into the attic and began sifting through the piles of papers. There were canceled checks, mortgage notices, and even high school love letters that represented parts of my father's and grandparents' lives.

In South Carolina it gets hot in August. There was a certain musty smell in the barn's attic, but the reading was fascinating and I stayed there most of the day. I found missing pieces of my father's life I hadn't known existed. Marshall Sanford married at an age older than most, and when we kids came along, he smothered us with attention.

During my high school track and cross-country races he was at every finish line. He was at my brothers' soccer games. Dad taught us how to barbecue chicken on the grill, how to run a farm tractor, and how to brand a cow. Most of all, he was just there for us.

Through new eyes, I began to see another side of my father. There were letters from his high school sweethearts, from the woman he would later marry, and from professional colleagues. A hundred of his dreams seemed to be sketched on the various pieces of paper I found, including his plans to build a home and the seemingly endless records of other projects. I was fascinated by it all.

I was caught very much off guard when I stumbled across an untitled folder my mom had kept. As I began to read the letters, it was clear they did not belong with the others. Everything was about my father's funeral. In my hand was a poem that my youngest brother, John, had written in February 1983, about three months after my father's death. I had never read it before, and I stopped to take in the words John had written.

The sunlight wakes as a new day is born,
The long day of my father has begun without scorn.
While the love of his work pushes him on,
The great love to his family keeps him strong.

While the conquest of excellence pushes him hard,
Great talent and dedication was his very best card.
All those who knew him while life was still his,
Would say in an instant, "The best surgeon to live."

The days of life that he wanted to know,
Suddenly became numbered, and then to go.
With his head up high, his mind strongly set,
He challenged each day while never upset.

So here is a man whose courage filled the seas,
and as I thank God for him, I drop to my knees.

I also discovered the ink-stained and mildewed pages from the eulogy our preacher, Frank Sells, gave on the day of my father's funeral. In part, it reads,

Several years ago, Marshall stopped by my office to inform his pastor about the things going on in his life. It was then he informed me of the disease which he thought would eventually take his life.

He talked about many things that morning, many alternatives. . . . I remember quoting to him the words of an atheist philosopher "Teach me how to die and I will teach you how to live." I asked Marshall if that was enough of a challenge. "Yes it is, but quite negative, Frank." He continued, "I prefer to accept the challenge of my Master, who said 'I have come to give you life. Life in all its abundance.' I prefer to accept that life, live that life in all of its fullness. I intend not to miss anything. I want to smell, to taste, to farm, to enjoy my family. I want to be an avid spectator, I want to worship my God in everything that I do." And that is exactly what Marshall Sanford did. He lived that way to the end. He lived with such intensity, such vigor, that everyone was touched. He hoped that his life could be lived thusly: "Let your light so shine before men, that they may see your good works and glorify your Father in heaven" (Matt. 5:16).

My eyes began to get teary as a flood of memories from fifteen years ago jumped forward to embrace me. I knew I had to tell my oldest son, Marshall, about the grandfather he never knew but whose name he carries.

My dad was the youngest of four children, with two brothers and a sister. He was born in a quiet and sleepy small town named Mocksville in the rolling hills of North Carolina between Winston-Salem and Statesville. Dad's perseverance, rather than sheer intellect, took him from Davie High School and Davidson College in North Carolina to the world-famous Johns Hopkins Medical School. Medicine was Dad's passion, and he threw his heart and soul into it. He became the chief resident for one of the original teams of heart surgery pioneers.

He fared well in the South Pacific during World War II, serving four years as surgeon on a military medical team. The intensity of medical school and the war made the years fly. It was not until he was forty that he met and married a thoughtful and elegant woman by the name of Margaret Pitz, who soon became my mother. The next thing Dad knew, he was the father of four children. I am the oldest, followed by Billy, Sarah, and John. Dad began private medical practice in Florida, built our home there, and purchased the farm he had always dreamed of owning in South Carolina.

Many successes came his way, largely because of sacrifices he and Mom made together for our common good. I am certain Dad's success as a father and a physician was the direct result of his ingrained perseverance.

As a boy I hadn't noticed the strength of my father's perseverance. In the winter of my junior year in high school, that changed. I had gone with Mom to the Miami Airport to pick up Dad, who was returning from a trip. As we drove the fifty miles toward home, Dad began to cry. Then Mom began to cry, too. Unexplainedly, he talked about how he didn't want to miss my graduation from high school, much less college; how he wanted to see me marry and have children; and how he wanted so much to watch me and my siblings grow to adulthood.

A few moments later Dad revealed that a fellow physician's diagnosis of his condition had been confirmed by the Mayo Clinic. Lou Gehrig's disease, named after the famous ballplayer who had it. The medical term is amyotrophic lateral sclerosis, better known as ALS. The terminal disease causes a slow and progressive wasting away of the body's muscles until its victim dies.

Dad was an astute doctor, and he knew what lay ahead for him. We would wait to tell my younger brothers and sister until arrangements were made to sell the house in Florida and move to the farm in South Carolina. If what the Mayo Clinic had suggested was true, Dad had about six months to live, and he wanted to spend his last days on the farm. I have vivid memories of that last battle of his life. The six-month prognosis turned into four years. I know his incredible perseverance, laced with prayer, delayed Dad's death. He fought against his growing disabilities through the final days of his life, trying to live each day to its fullest.

Shortly after the diagnosis, he lost the intricate use of his hands that was needed to perform delicate heart surgery. Rather than sit around and do nothing, Dad searched for things he was capable of doing. At first, he drove the farm's tractor and operated the more complex pieces of machinery. Toward the end, Dad drove a bulldozer. It is actually one of the simpler pieces of equipment to drive, mostly pushing and pulling levers and stepping on pedals. He loved to clear land. I figure he envisioned his sons, or maybe his grandchildren, would someday raise cattle or plant a crop on the land he had cleared.

Early in the morning of each day, my brother and I helped Dad into the pickup truck and drove him to the edge of the field. After we helped him out of the pickup, he began to walk toward the bulldozer. Land recently cleared is called new ground, and it is often rough and broken. Dad's steps had become short and choppy. He lost his balance and fell facedown in the South Carolina soil.

My brother and I reached forward to help him, picking him up and brushing the dirt from his clothes. Indignant, he said to us, "I want to do it myself!" We did as we were told. He took a few more steps and fell down. We lifted him up, and he began again. That sequence was repeated several times on his way to the bulldozer, and after he successfully arrived, we could see the sense of accomplishment in his smile. There are other stories our family could tell from those four years of Dad's fight with ALS, and all would have a common thread. Dad just wouldn't give up. As his physical condition reduced his activity to a lower level, he found new things he could accomplish at that level.

It was on Thanksgiving night of my senior year in college, with Mom and his four children at his side, that Dad died. Though he knew he was dying, he never talked much about it, and my brothers and I tried to deny he was going to die. Never one for fanfare, Dad hoped he could be buried in a plain pine box in one of the fields he cleared with his bulldozer.

My brothers and I were proud to honor that request. I built the coffin from a South Carolina pine that grew on the farm. My brothers prepared the grave beneath two huge oak trees; his wreath was the Spanish moss on their branches that waved gently back and forth when breezes rolled in from the nearby river. He would have loved the service. Most of all, Dad would have wanted that I pass along the value of persevering to our three young sons, Marshall, Landon, and Bolton, who one day, I hope, will know the meaning of perseverance that is not spoken, but lived, each day of life.

Through observing my dad's daily life, I came to learn how true is this quotation by Calvin Coolidge: "Nothing in the world can take the place of persistence. Talent will not; nothing is more common than unsuccessful men with talent. Genius will not; unrewarded genius is almost a proverb. Education will not; the world is full of educated derelicts. Persistence and determination are omnipotent. The slogan 'press on' has solved and always will solve the problems of the human race." My prayer for Marshall, Landon, and Bolton is that they will not just read or talk about perseverance, but they will possess it as well. What matters is the kind of perseverance their grandfather possessed and the way he lived because of it.

As I sit at my desk and reflect on the months that have flown by since I became a member of Congress, I realize the importance of perseverance in my life. The necessity of this unseen attribute became clear as I watched issues I supported, such as term limits, come to the House floor for a vote and go down in defeat. It is obvious to me that in my dad's way of thinking that means try, try, and try again.

I feel fortunate to have had a father who gave me a living example of what it means to persevere.

CONGRESSWOMAN
LINDA SMITH

CONGRESS OF THE UNITED STATES
HOUSE OF REPRESENTATIVES

THE THIRD DISTRICT OF WASHINGTON

Congresswoman Smith has earned the distinction of being the first person in Washington state history to qualify for a congressional general election ballot as a write-in candidate.

Smith has a record of public service going back to 1983, when she was elected to the Washington state house of representatives. She was reelected in 1984 and 1986. In 1987, she was victorious in a Washington state senate special election against an appointed incumbent and was re-elected in 1988 and 1992. Smith served in several leadership positions during her senate tenure. She authored the Fair Campaign Practices Act, a major campaign and ethics reform initiative that was overwhelmingly approved by voters in 1993. She was also the author of Initiative 601, which placed a limit on state expenditures and taxes.

For fourteen years Smith operated a tax consulting business. She and her husband, Vern, have two children and six grandchildren. Her scenic Third District encompasses the cities of Vancouver and Olympia, Washington.

Congresswoman Smith serves on the Resources Committee and the Small Business Committee. She is a member of four subcommittees and is the chairwoman of the Small Business Subcommittee on Taxation and Finance.

How to Contact

> 1217 Longworth House Office Building,
> Washington, D.C. 20515
> Telephone: 202-225-3536
> Fax: 202-225-3478

☆ ☆ ☆ ☆ ☆ ☆ ☆ ☆ ☆ ☆ ☆ ☆ ☆

A framed quotation from Abraham Lincoln sits on the desk of my Washington, D.C., office. It speaks to me often:

> *I am not bound to win,*
> *but I am bound to be true.*
> *I am not bound to succeed,*
> *but I am bound to live up to what light I have.*
> *I must stand with anybody that stands right,*
> *and part with him when he goes wrong.*

These are simple words from a seemingly simple man, yet they have the power to inspire me when I need it most—whether at the start of a full day of difficult meetings, just before I go to the House floor to cast a tough vote, or after the loss of the battle on a hard-fought amendment.

All of us have someone who has influenced our lives, whether as close as a mother or as distant as a figure from history one hundred thirty years ago. Often, we extract our most admired traits not from one person but from a myriad of people. If I had to name only one person who embodies all that I hold in high esteem, it would be Abraham Lincoln. He is the string-bean country lawyer who worked his way from poverty to politics.

Lincoln staked his claim in American history by becoming the first Republican president, one who brought his wounded nation through a bloody civil war intact. He possessed the steadfastness and courage necessary to do what was right in an era when what was right was not popular. Lincoln never abandoned his beliefs and was true to himself throughout his life: *"I am not bound to win, but I am bound to be true."* Abraham Lincoln was not a politician for the politicians. He was a people's politician. Coming from humble roots, with a little luck and a lot of persistence, he learned a lawyer's trade and eventually found his way to the U.S. capital not by design but by destiny.

Lincoln championed the not-so-popular idea of ending slavery. In the mid-nineteenth century, many of the politically elite owned slaves. Owning slaves was socially acceptable and economically vital to many people. "It's our way of life; stay out of it," slave owners warned the abolitionists. In the volatile political climate of the 1850s, local and national leaders were in cahoots with the Supreme Court. Shortly before the Civil War, the Court had ruled that slaves were to be considered property and therefore could be denied the rights of free people. They could be bought and sold like any other commodity.

Despite all the social indicators to the contrary, Lincoln knew it was wrong to treat African-Americans like nonhumans. His position was not easy to defend, and many of Lincoln's peers rejected and alienated him. People often ridiculed him for standing alone in his conviction, yet he refused to conform and make things easier for himself. In his heart, Lincoln knew he was right, and the hindsight of history validates his actions.

Children reading history books ask their teachers, "Did white people really own black people?" This way of life, considered the norm when Lincoln assumed the presidency, is considered nothing less than deplorable today. Often, many of my freshman colleagues and I find ourselves in a position similar to Lincoln's. For example, ever since some of us decided to publicly defend the rights of unborn Americans, powerful social forces have been pushing and pulling at us to modify our convictions.

Constantly rowing against the current is difficult and tiring, but I have learned that you draw strength from knowing that where you're going is the right destination. A statement in the Scriptures reveals that God has placed in the human heart the knowledge of good and evil, but some allow that knowledge to be overcome by the force of opinion. I suppose for many it's easy to let go of the thorny issue and let their boats float along on the tide, just not saying or doing anything at all.

Good and decent people do this all the time. While quietly resolving not to rock the boat, they fail to recognize they have rocked their conscience to sleep. As Lincoln alerted his colleagues and the American people to a grievous wrong, many of us in the 104th Congress are trying to do the same with the issues we face today. *"I must stand with anybody that stands right, and part with him when he goes wrong."* When push came to shove, and then a downright free-for-all, Lincoln went to war over slavery. The Southern states refused to free their slaves, but he wanted freedom for all. There were no options available; the choice was to fight or witness the dissolution of the nation.

Some people urged deliberation and a slower pace. "You can't do it all at once," they cautioned, but Lincoln was not swayed. As painful as it was to see his beloved country divided, with brothers fighting against brothers, he would not be deterred from his course. The Emancipation Proclamation, signed by Lincoln in January 1863, freed the slaves permanently and gave substance to Lincoln's vision of freedom for every American. In 1865, the Civil War ended, and the solidarity of our nation was preserved.

Believing that one person could make a difference, I ran for the state house and challenged the incumbent during a special election. Few thought it could be done, but with the help of tremendous grassroots support, I won! Four years later I found myself in the same situation, but the race was for a state senate seat. As before, there were plenty of doubting Thomases, and again I won. I wanted to stay there, serving the voters in Washington state.

On Labor Day 1994, the leading Republican contender in my Third Congressional District dropped out of the race. My husband, Vern, and I returned from a weekend trip and were welcomed home to an organized write-in campaign that was already in the works by my hard-driving supporters. It was Linda Smith for Congress! It wasn't up to me anymore; it was up to the people of the Third District.

We had less than two weeks to get my name on the primary ballot. Community activists from all over my district came together and worked side by side, putting mailers together, calling voters, and erecting signs throughout the district. The naysayers were out in full force, but they were proven wrong by the power of the voting booth. Because of the indefatigable efforts of my boosters, I became the first congressperson in state history to win an election as a write-in candidate.

Seven weeks later in the general election, I defeated a three-term incumbent, and Vern and I were on our way to Washington! On our way to what, exactly, we didn't know. Washington, D.C., was as foreign to me as it is to most Americans, but I would soon learn. *"I am not bound to succeed, but I am bound to live up to what light I have."*

Taking a stand on an issue is part of being in politics. Where others may keep their views quiet, even secret, elected officials are denied that option. Members of the media will always make sure a congressperson's opinions are publicized for all to see, especially if they seem controversial. We must search our souls for answers to issues affecting all Americans, ranging from the public to the private. After we have found an answer, sticking to it sometimes doesn't garner the popular vote.

We are fast learning where the battle lines are drawn on pro-life issues, on balancing the national budget, and on passing campaign finance reform. We are hearing the same obstructive excuse Lincoln heard so long ago: "You can't do it all at once." A few things must be done all at once, or they likely will never be done at all. Contrary to what some believe, real change does often occur overnight and not in bits and pieces. The congressional elections of 1994 that overturned a forty-year Democratic stranglehold on Congress happened in the space of a single election day. This proves that if the people's motivation is great enough, positive change can take place in hours or days, not years.

Political lessons often come in a startling fashion to a freshman congressperson. In my first year in Congress, I offered my first major amendment on the historic floor of the House of Representatives. It was to eliminate a $23 million tobacco subsidy for crop insurance and extension services. Taxpayers don't want their money propping up a dangerous product like tobacco, I thought, and Congress is looking for ways to balance the budget. It seemed like one of the right places to start, a no-brainer, as my grandkids would say. Cosponsors of the amendment were Representatives Hansen (R-Utah) and Durbin (D-Illinois). We split up and began to work the floor, attempting to rally support for our cause. The gavel fell fifteen minutes later when the House clerk called for a vote. It was 199 for, versus 223 against. We had lost!

As I sat there in my seat pondering the outcome, I grew more and more angry. How could two of the House's most conservative members and one of its most liberal, join in a rare bipartisan fashion and then lose a vote that had such strong support from the American people? Did we fall victim to a system that rewards the highest bidder, the tobacco industry? Had another good idea been scuttled in a flood of campaign contributions received at night-after-night special interest fund-raisers for incumbents in Washington?

The amendment we put forward was an attempt to reach a balanced budget, but its defeat was not in vain. It shined a bright light on the need for campaign reform. If I accomplish nothing else in Congress, it will be to help end a system that is failing the American people. That's why a group of congressional reformers have introduced a bill to remove the tainted influence of cash showered on Congress by special interests and bring the focus of future campaigns home, to our citizenry. The American people will not begin to trust Congress until their representatives have taken the money out of the decision-making process in Washington.

We are convinced campaign reform is the right thing to do, but a strong current is moving against us. Some say we should study the issue more. Perhaps they have never heard that "analysis is paralysis." Others tell me it's been this way for years; don't disrupt it. Incredulously, some have said it's legal, so there's nothing to worry about!

Does this sound familiar?

It will take all the determination we can muster to get a campaign reform bill passed through Congress. Although many of our freshman members are real bulldogs, they are up against the entrenched habits of an older political lifestyle. It will take steadfastness and courage. It will take the tenacity to keep standing for what we believe is right when most everyone else is too tired to stand any longer.

Working together, serious congressional political reformers can make the current system of campaigning become a part of American history. I want to live in a future where children will ask their teachers in disbelief, "Did politicians really take money when they voted?"

Through sheer force of will, Lincoln was able to hold his country together through a bloody and divisive civil war. With God's help, I believe our citizens' confidence can be restored in our federal government by diligently applying the force of our will to the problems before us.

CONGRESSMAN MARK SOUDER

CONGRESS OF THE UNITED STATES
HOUSE OF REPRESENTATIVES

THE FOURTH DISTRICT OF INDIANA

A native of Fort Wayne, Souder attended public schools and graduated from Indiana University with a bachelor of science degree in business administration. He received his master's degree from the University of Notre Dame Graduate School of Business.

Representative Souder's great-great-grandfather settled in Allen County, Indiana, in 1846. He was one of the first Amish settlers in the county. His family founded Souder's of Grabill in 1907. The original harness shop grew into a series of family businesses. Souder is president of Historic Souder's of Grabill.

In 1983, Souder served as economic development liaison for Representative Dan Coats. In 1984, Representative Coats appointed Souder to be Republican staff director of the House Select Committee on Children, Youth, and Families. When Coats was appointed to the United States Senate in 1989, Souder served as his legislative director and deputy chief of staff until returning to Fort Wayne in 1993.

Souder and his wife, the former Diane Zimmer, live in Fort Wayne with their three children, Brooke, Nathan, and Zachary. They attend Emmanuel Community Church. Souder is also a member of the Grabill Chamber of Commerce.

Congressman Souder's freshmen colleagues elected him class vice president for the 104th Congress. He is a member of the Economic and Educational Opportunities, Government Reform and Oversight, and Small Business Committees. He serves on six subcommittees.

How to Contact

508 Cannon House Office Building,
Washington, D.C. 20515
Telephone: 202-225-4436
Fax: 202-225-3479

☆ ☆ ☆ ☆ ☆ ☆ ☆ ☆ ☆ ☆ ☆ ☆ ☆ ☆

We need more of the office desk and less of the show-window in politics. Let men in office substitute the midnight oil for the lime-light.

—President Calvin Coolidge

I n Washington, D.C., many people and institutions think highly of themselves. A major bank advertises its existence as "the most important bank in the most important city in the world," illustrating that humility is not our capital city's greatest virtue. Coming to Washington as a freshman congressperson seldom develops desirable virtues such as humility. If you don't arrive instilled with solid character values, chances are, you won't take any with you when you leave.

The history of our American presidency is filled with models of arrogance and pride, but not much humility. Although I like the laid-back styles of Presidents Ronald Reagan and Abraham Lincoln, my favorite president is Calvin Coolidge. Not only because he lowered taxes and balanced the federal budget, just as we are trying to do today, but because Washington's power politics and the isolation of the White House did not blind him to the needs of people in a lesser station.

Coolidge's White House social secretary recalled a story about an admirer who said she did not see how the president could bear up under all his pressing responsibilities and she prayed often for his good health and guidance. She inquired whether Coolidge did not feel the burden was more than he could endure. Coolidge casually quipped, "Oh, I don't know. There are only so many hours in the day, and one can only do the best he can in the time he's got. When I was mayor of Northampton I was pretty busy most of the time, and I don't seem to be much busier here. I just have to settle different kinds of things."

Incoming President Herbert Hoover wrote that Coolidge

passed on some fatherly advice to him on how to run the White House and deal with the daily nuances of being president. Coolidge advised, "You have to stand every day three or four hours of visitors. Nine-tenths of them want something they ought not to have. If you keep dead still they will run-down in three or four minutes, if you even cough or smile they will start up all over again."

When Coolidge was lieutenant governor of Massachusetts, a man coming out of his office was asked if Coolidge was there. He sarcastically replied, "There was a man in there that looked something like his picture, who said nothing and was apparently not paying much attention." Biographer Edward Elwell Whiting went on with the story, reporting that the men met two weeks later and the one who made the comment about Coolidge had changed his opinion, offering this update: "That man Coolidge is a star. I thought he was paying no attention. I was wrong. I find that he wrote at once to Plymouth to learn all the facts, he went personally to the wharves, talked with the pilots of Boston harbor, learned about the duties of a pilot, and he now has worked out a plan for correcting the troubles at Plymouth."

Calvin Coolidge may have been "Silent Cal," but he had an unseen sense of duty. He felt that if he did his job well, future opportunities would arise. If not, then at least he did his job well. Not only did critics grant that Coolidge had humility, and no apparent driving ambition, but many of his frustrated supporters felt the same way! He climbed up the ladder of politics in the classic textbook manner, first a city official, then state representative, mayor, state senator, majority leader, lieutenant governor, governor, vice president of the United States, and president. His political career parallels the modern corporate Cinderella story, in which the chairman of the board started in the mailroom and quietly worked his way to the top.

Coolidge campaigned aggressively while crediting God's

larger plan for him. Commentators observed that when he was elected vice president, if they were President Harding, they would quit so they wouldn't suddenly die in office. Ironically, that is exactly what happened when Warren G. Harding died in 1923, and our constitutional process elevated Calvin Coolidge to the highest office in the land, the thirtieth president of the United States. Called "Coolidge's luck" by many, his inheritance of a higher position would have more credence if it happened once or twice, but it happened over and over during his long tour as a public official.

As World War I was coming to a bloody end in 1918, Coolidge gave us a glimpse into his deep conviction about the importance of self-sacrifice to advance society:

> The law of progress and civilization is not the law of the jungle. It is not an earthly law, it is a divine law. It does not mean the survival of the fittest, it means the sacrifice of the fittest. Any mother will give her life for her child. Men put women and children into lifeboats before they themselves will leave the sinking ship. John Hampden and Nathan Hale did not survive, nor did Lincoln, but Benedict Arnold did. The example above all other takes us back to Jerusalem some nineteen hundred years ago.

There were undoubtedly many reasons why Calvin Coolidge became the man described by eulogists and historians. A recent author explained Coolidge's "bond with the cobbler, the delivery man, the grocer, the news vendor, the druggist, even the tavern keeper. Ordinary people felt that Coolidge with his rustic, small-town background rooted in Vermont, was more like them and not condescending like most politicians." President Coolidge came from a tiny village that even sixty years ago was unflatteringly called a "waxworks museum" by essayist William Allen White. Calvin's mom died when he was young, as did his sister. His father was a man of few words, and he may have been the model for the young Coolidge's reluctance to dominate a conversation.

The most significant event ever to occur in Plymouth Notch was the swearing in of Calvin Coolidge as president, after learning of Harding's death that evening. Because his father was a justice of the peace, and thus a federal official, it is the only administration of a presidential oath conducted by the president's father. Years later, when Coolidge, Sr., was asked how he knew he could give the presidential oath of office to his son, he answered, "Well, I didn't know I couldn't." In Coolidgespeak, that meant several books and sources had been checked that said "federal official," and none of them excluded a justice of the peace, though some people thought that interpretation was a bit of a stretch. His father may not have been much of a talker, but he made a lasting impression on Cal. He wrote in his autobiography, "My father, John Calvin Coolidge, ran the country store. He was successful. I was exceedingly anxious to grow up to be like him." That is the ultimate compliment a son can pay a father.

As someone who has read biographies of most of the American presidents, I point out that the family relationships of many presidents have been dicey at best. Calvin was an admirable exception, and his devotion to family was made clear in this touching story from his stepmother, Carrie Brown Coolidge. "I suppose Calvin is a very busy man," she commented to a visitor. The visitor confirmed that he was, and Mrs. Coolidge continued, "I want to tell you something about him. No mother ever had a better son than Calvin has been to me, and you know, I am not his own mother. Never a week goes by without a letter from him. Often he writes two or three times a week. I do not believe many boys write to their mothers like that."

Coolidge also preached what he practiced. His speeches, made over a decades-long political career, are amazingly consistent. In them, he frequently referred to what he called the "homely virtues." In a message to Congress in December 1923, Coolidge expounded his belief that the home is the cradle of moral development. He urged, "Mere intelligence is not enough. Enlightenment must be accompanied by that moral power which is the product of home and of religion. Real education and true welfare for the people rest inevitably on this foundation, which the government can approve and command, but which the people themselves must create."

Some will contend that Coolidge's humility was well deserved. It is true he was not the suave or glamorous leader that Washington society and media pundits prefer. To say he was humble was not to say he lacked confidence, but it is difficult for many to believe the two traits could go hand in hand. When beginning his law practice, the young Coolidge wrote his father, "And I can say in all meekness that Hardy is the only one who can grasp a question of law as well as I can." Another point often ignored by critics is that someone doesn't subject himself to the potential embarrassment of electoral defeat if he lacks self-confidence. Yet in all the elected positions he held, Coolidge retained his hometown style of humility.

With the possible exception of Abraham Lincoln, humility has not been a presidential icon. It seems hard to find a kid elected to one term as student council president who has humility about what he has achieved. Coolidge worked to pass this trait on to his sons. When one of his boys was working in the fields of western Massachusetts, another boy told him if his father was president, he wouldn't be working so hard. Young Coolidge retorted, "You would be if your father were my father."

Grace Coolidge was a good match for Calvin. She was as socially adept as her husband was silent, and she had a wide-eyed wonder that was appealing. When Grace was still single, she chaperoned a number of high school pupils on a sightseeing trip to Washington, D.C. As she toured the White House, she could not resist touching the valuable gold piano in the East Room and a guard ordered her to move on, but the chance to touch the piano was just too great a temptation. Laughing, she predicted to the guard, "Someday I'll come back here, open that piano and play it, and you won't order me out!"

The Coolidges never changed from their simple Vermont upbringing, and though becoming more worldly, Calvin retained his original values. At Amherst College he was remembered as a student "not for what he did or said, but by the principles by which he lives, the qualities he displayed and the character that he was." Later, when asked of his goals as governor of Massachusetts, he typically explained, "To walk humbly and discharge my obligations."

Coolidge wrote his own speeches, which was a bit unusual even in the 1920s. Detractors said they were simple and full of cliches. Coolidge artfully replied, "They criticize me for harping on the obvious. Perhaps someday I'll write on *The Importance of the Obvious*. If all the folks in the United States would do the few simple things they know they ought to do, most of our big problems would take care of themselves."

Coolidge was very well read. He didn't spend his free time talking; he spent it reading. When faced with problems as a legislator, he was known for detailed and personal research that formed his opinions. He attended meetings and actually listened to both sides. It wasn't that he didn't understand that people made complicated arguments to prove their point. He believed that finding solutions revolved around grasping the underlying principles of the dispute.

If you understand the personal Coolidge, you will understand the political Coolidge. He was not a particularly religious man in the sense of regular church attendance and daily worship, and he was a classic New England–style Puritan. That is, life is not supposed to be fun; it is full of duty, obligations, and things that must be accomplished, and God has an overall plan that we are here to fulfill.

Because of the dedicated belief that God has a higher moral plan for humankind, Coolidge did not think that people would suddenly change the world. If the virtuous behavior of individuals was to be preeminent, Coolidge would not be convinced that government could be the major solution to human problems. Both beliefs led to personal humility. Conversely, if people believe that they can change the world and there are no higher virtues that transcend their own, they are not likely to be very humble.

This comment demonstrates how Coolidge applied his philosophy about virtues: "There are others which are more insidious, more dangerous, which come under the guise of government activity instigated for the general good." A sense of duty gave Coolidge courage. His defining political moment was the Boston police strike, when as governor he ordered the National Guard to restore order with the famous remark, "There is no right to strike against the public safety by anybody, anywhere, anytime." This defiance of a local uprising made Coolidge a national figure, soon to be nominated as the Republican vice presidential contender.

Other Republicans disagreed with his action, even while he was signing the order to mobilize the National Guard. They told him if he signed, he would probably destroy the Republican Party in Massachusetts and forever make it impossible to hold any other elective office. The governor looked at them, pen in hand, and said quietly, "Perhaps you are right," and he affixed his signature to the document. There was no yelling, arguing, or grandstanding. Calvin Coolidge humbly did what he thought was the right thing. If a man feels soundly anchored in family, home, and God, he has special courage that others cannot muster.

Massachusetts House Speaker Gillett nominated Calvin Coolidge for president with this testimony:

Just to do his duty well has been his life's characteristic. He is not showy or spectacular, but he never disappoints. A poor man, living in the most frugal simplicity, he always had the confidence and support of the working people, yet rich and poor are to him alike, equal before the law. He never crooks the pregnant hinges of the knee before pretentious power, nor stiffens his neck in pride before lowly weakness, but he holds the even tenor of his upright way, following his polestar of duty.

People can do little to prepare for the viciousness of politics. Many of us contributing to this book have been subjected to smears on our personal lives. Anyone aspiring to elected office faces not only public dissertations on every mistake ever made, but the media and opponents may be counted upon to distort them. Politics is not for the faint of heart. I am thankful for the examples set for me by my parents who sacrificed much for me; for the Americans who sacrificed so that we might live as free citizens today; and most of all for Jesus Christ whose sacrifice washed away all our sins. My friend Sharon Soderstrom often quotes her father, Karl, longtime headmaster of the prestigious Stony Brook School on Long Island, as saying, "You can serve Him anywhere."

One of the greatest honors in being part of this freshman class in Congress is seeing so many of my fellow members of Congress with this sense of humility possessed by Calvin Coolidge and based on their solid personal values. From this inner strength comes the special courage to challenge an entrenched political bureaucracy and, if necessary, our leadership. It is my prayer that we can be joined in Washington and throughout America by people who are committed to serving God in this great nation. Calvin Coolidge said it well in a college address in 1923:

> We do not need more intellectual power, we need more
>   moral power.

We do not need more knowledge, we need more character.
We do not need more government, we need more culture.
We do not need more law, we need more religion.
We do not need more of the things that are seen,
    we need more of the things that are unseen.
If the foundation be firm, the foundation will stand.

I am privileged to serve in the United States Congress, and there could not be a more exciting time to be here. We have a group of motivated freshmen, rooted in the values I have extolled in Calvin Coolidge. We may not win every battle, but we have hope in our hearts that what is right and best for our nation will prevail.

CONGRESSMAN
STEVE STOCKMAN

CONGRESS OF THE UNITED STATES
HOUSE OF REPRESENTATIVES

THE NINTH DISTRICT OF TEXAS

In November 1994, enthusiastic grassroots support for Steve Stockman ended the forty-two-year congressional career of his opponent and earned Stockman the title of Newsmaker of the Year for 1994. Congressman Stockman came to the House of Representatives with a vision of limiting federal government, strongly supporting American families, and achieving a balanced budget.

During the first one hundred days, Stockman strove to reduce the size and scope of the federal government, starting with Congress itself. As sponsor of the Dreier/Stockman package of opening day reforms, Stockman dramatically pared down the hierarchy of the House by eliminating three full House committees and twenty-three subcommittees and by cutting committee staff by one-third.

Recently, journalists around the country have heralded Stockman for being a leader, and he has appeared on the *McNeil-Lehrer News Hour* to discuss the Mexican bailout situation.

At home, Stockman is active in community affairs, focusing his attention on youth and education. He has served as a member of the board of directors for the Hugh O'Brien Youth Foundation and worked with the South Texas Leadership Conference, for which he and his wife, Patti, have been counselors. They are members of the First Baptist Church of Houston.

Stockman's Ninth District consists of the cities of Galveston, Baytown, Beaumont, Port Arthur, Texas City, and the Clear Lake area. Primary economic supporters of the district are NASA's Johnson Space Center and the oil and gas industries along the Texas Gulf shoreline.

Congressman Stockman serves on the Science Committee and the Banking and Financial Services Committee and is a member of four subcommittees.

How to Contact

417 Cannon House Office Building,
Washington, D.C. 20515
Telephone: 202-225-6565

☆ ☆ ☆ ☆ ☆ ☆ ☆ ☆ ☆ ☆ ☆ ☆ ☆

Commitment is a word used in many ways. People say they cannot do something because they have a previous commitment. Some people commit crimes. If you are a dangerous person, you may be committed. One of the most sublime meanings in the English language belongs to the word *commitment*. If you have a personal commitment, you pledge your name to a cause and allow your beliefs to dictate your actions, which may be neither easy nor comfortable. The Lone Star State is home for more than its share of men and women who let their beliefs guide their actions, some of whom paid for their commitment with their very lives. If people should die because of their commitment to freedom, they are rightly called heroes. One such man was Davy Crockett.

To paraphrase a popular country song, "my heroes have always been Texans." Growing up in Michigan, I learned about Texas from the source for all young boys who desire higher learning: the movies! John Wayne taught me more about the history of Texas than any American history class. I still admire early heroes Stephen Austin, Sam Houston, William B. Travis, and Jim Bowie and the modern heroes of my generation, the astronauts at NASA. These natural leaders fired my imagination as nothing else could. However, one name stands out to me as the ultimate Texan, which at first may seem strange since he lived nearly his entire life in other places, yet he answered the desperate call to defend the state's freedom. That man was commitment personified; he was Davy Crockett.

I find the similarities between Crockett and myself nothing short of remarkable. Crockett was born on a hilltop in Tennessee, while I was born in Bloomfield Hills, Michigan. His was the greenest state in the land of the free; mine was the brownest. He killed his first bear when he was only three, I ate my first Gummi Bear when I was only three! Seriously, the similarities do not end there. Davy Crockett came to Texas from another state to advance the cause of freedom, and he has been a model that led me from Michigan to Texas and finally to Congress.

Davy was born in 1786 to John Crockett, a soldier in the American Revolution, who fought at the battle of King's Mountain. John was an extremely strict father, and at age thirteen Davy ran away from his parents' Tennessee home to avoid a whipping by his dad. He wandered the forested hills of Tennessee for three years, and upon returning home, he volunteered to pay off the debts accumulated by his father. He demonstrated his commitment to the family even at the age of sixteen, exhibiting a capacity beyond his years, by forgiving his father for past injustices.

For me, the idea of commitment to family is paramount. My commitment to the American family inspired me to run for public office. When I saw what the policies of our federal government were doing to our families, children, and communities, I knew I had to let my beliefs dictate my actions. Fighting for the betterment of the American family through my efforts in Congress has been the way to make my feet follow my heart.

At the advanced age of eighteen, Crockett went to school. His attendance was not for receiving an education, but for wooing a young woman! Though not "book smart," he was a man with a natural facility for making plans and carrying them out. Unfortunately, the young woman he was courting was won away by another. Not to be deterred at love, Crockett quickly made a different choice, married, and began a family.

Davy and Polly Crockett first tried farming near his parents' home in Tennessee, but Davy's skills at hunting did not spill over into farming, and the farm failed. The Crockett family, with two babies, moved to a more suitable region of Tennessee. Crockett did not complain about the tough times or ask for a government program to retrain displaced frontiersmen. Instead, he picked himself up, moved down the road, and started over. Perhaps

Crockett's strongest commitment was to self-help. Before America adopted the programs of the Great Society, it was not a nation asking the federal government, like a child crying to his mother, to dry its tears and wipe its nose.

During the Creek War of 1813, Crockett served with distinction as a scout under the direction of General Andy Jackson, not realizing he was reporting to a future president of the United States. He took most seriously his responsibility to our young nation. His commitment to America dictated he do his duty, although he personally disliked General Jackson. These were difficult times for Crockett. The next year his wife died, and he was left with three youngsters. Always resourceful, he soon married the widow of a fellow soldier and moved his newly formed family about eighty miles west. His leadership skills became evident, and he was chosen to be the local magistrate, followed by his appointment to justice of the peace, where he boasted that his decisions "relied on natural-born sense instead of law learning." His devotion to an American system of citizen-judges was emblematic of a time in American history that allowed competent and respected men to adjudicate issues. In other words, not every trial was turned into a federal case, and common sense prevailed.

In those days, every state had organized volunteers to preserve order, and Crockett was elected colonel to lead the local armed volunteers. Riding his rising popularity, he was elected to the Tennessee state legislature. While there, he voted for a bill to pay a pension to widows of soldiers killed in the war. A constituent wrote to Crockett and put forth the premise that that amounted to stealing from one citizen to give to another. When Crockett read that, he believed it was true, and he was so remorseful about his earlier support of the bill, he immediately went to the floor of the statehouse and denounced the pension. Knowing that the widows still needed help, he then took up a collection from the legislators to pay them a stipend. Crockett gave generously.

His commitment to being a citizen-soldier and a citizen-legislator has applications today when it seems only career politicians and lawyers from Ivy League schools are comfortable leading our nation. Crockett's next move was to the westernmost point of Tennessee. His nearest neighbor was seven miles away. In the wilderness isolation, he became a legend as a bear hunter. Unlike today, in the early nineteenth century, there was no shortage of bears. He once claimed, and there is no reason to doubt him, that he killed 105 bears in eight months.

After tiring of killing bears, Crockett went after dumber animals. In 1826, he ran for Congress, employing a campaign that mixed humor with sincerity. His animated stories of frontier courage excited the crowds. So what did his two opponents do? They ran mean-spirited campaigns that ridiculed Crockett and his homespun ways. It did not work; the voters saw through the personal attacks and elected him to Congress. That lesson was important to me in my race against forty-two-year incumbent Jack Brooks. While Brooks ran ads attacking me personally, I stayed positive. On election day the voters in my district saw through those personal attacks, just as voters had done nearly 170 years ago for Crockett, and I was elected to Congress.

In the 1830s a Jacksonian democracy swept across America. The wave also swept Crockett out of office, a backlash to his well-known dislike for Old Hickory. Incensed, he advised his former constituents, "I'm going to Texas!" Crockett then made a decision that would change the course of American history.

The far-off sounds of war were coming from Texas. The self-appointed dictator of Mexico, General Antonio Lopez de Santa Anna, had suspended the Mexican Constitution of 1824 that guaranteed Texas settlers equality with Mexican citizens. Santa Anna was a vile dictator who fancied himself the Napoleon of the

New World. He wanted to stop what was then the northern Mexican state of Texas from enjoying many personal liberties assumed throughout the United States and Mexico. Those rights were always guaranteed by the laws of Mexico. The citizens of Texas, drawn by Mexico's promise of good farming and protected liberties, wanted nothing more than a return to the Constitution of 1824.

Davy Crockett arrived in Texas leading a band of Tennessee volunteers and proceeded to an obscure Spanish mission in present-day San Antonio called the Alamo. On the way, an unusual thing happened; Crockett was in a fight with a cougar. After having one arm and a leg bitten by the big cat, he killed it with a knife. The next day he complained of soreness, but he was not going to let a mere mauling prevent him from participating in the fight for freedom.

Upon his arrival at the Alamo, Crockett found the old Spanish mission about to be attacked by the Mexican army under the leadership of Santa Anna, and he was immediately appointed to the rank of colonel. Inside the adobe walls, the Alamo regulars were commanded by Colonel William B. Travis, an educated man who insisted on maintaining military discipline. In contrast, the volunteers were a ragtag army led by Colonel James Bowie. Regardless of appearance, whether educated or illiterate, all the men were destined to die as heroes. Crockett's wit, his storytelling skill, and an unfailing ability to outfox dangerous adversaries had made him a living legend long before he arrived in Texas. The fact that he came from the safety of Tennessee, aptly nicknamed the Volunteer State, to fight for the freedom of people he had never met shows a nobleness of purpose that I strive to emulate.

If there is a temple to freedom, it is the Alamo. In that place, 187 Anglos, African-Americans, and Hispanics fought side by side to preserve the rights every human being should inherit. They stood against 6,500 Mexican soldiers who, if victorious, would take away the freedom of every Texan. The Alamo garrison knew the Mexican army was marching north to capture the mission.

Many heroic accounts have come from what those brave men and women did in their final days, but one story is irrefutable. Outnumbered thirty-five to one with few cannon and no reserves, Travis knew their chance of survival was zero. Still, if he could delay the advance of the Mexican army long enough, Sam Houston would have time to recruit and train a larger fighting force. Travis called for all to gather in the sandy courtyard, and unsheathing his sword, he scratched a long line in the sand. The colonel explained that the Mexican army was near, and the soldiers meant to kill everyone found in the fortress. Though death would be the inevitable outcome of remaining in the Alamo, he announced he was staying until the end.

Travis would make his stand in the Alamo to save the main army and perish so that Texas could be free. He looked over his troops, many just farmers who wanted to live free of the oppressive rule of Santa Anna. He revealed the strength of his commitment when he said, "Santa Anna is coming with his army. I won't hold it against anyone who wants to leave here. Many of you have families, and nobody will think you a coward for wanting to go home to them. I am staying, and any one of you who wants to stay and die for freedom, come and cross this line." Slowly at first and then in a wave, every man stepped forward and crossed the line drawn in the sand. Jim Bowie, on a stretcher and very ill, directed that his stretcher be lifted and carried across the line.

Crockett, as one would expect, gladly stepped over the line. I have always marveled at how the men so readily chose death over enslavement. They still had time and opportunity to escape, but they chose to die on their feet rather than live on their knees. All elected the same fate.

The first wave of the Mexican army went forward with an

arrogance that announced defeat would be impossible. But defeat came nonetheless, as the shrinking number of defenders held off the Mexican army from behind the sacred walls of the Alamo. For thirteen days, less than two hundred resolute Texans broke every charge and stopped every advance of the Mexican soldiers. Santa Anna sent his troops in waves against the pockmarked walls, indifferent to the carnage suffered by his conscripts. He commented to a worried subordinate that casualties did not matter because a soldier is like an ant, too plentiful to be of concern to a great general.

The Mexican Napoleon was unable to break the stubborn Texans' defense. With shouts of "come and take it," the cannoneers aimed their artillery directly into the oncoming mass, their deadly harvest causing Santa Anna to send for reinforcements. Thousands of Mexican soldiers were hastily recalled from their pursuit of Sam Houston's army to capture the tiny citadel of liberty. The precious gift of time granted the Texas army a respite and prepared them for the battle that assured Texas's independence, the Battle of San Jacinto.

After nearly two weeks of bloody fighting and thousands of Mexican casualties, the final and devastating assault on the battered fortress occurred. Every defender was killed, but the price for Santa Anna was much higher. Two thousand of his troops were dead and many more incapacitated by wounds, but the main army of Texas was safe. The Alamo fell, and the idea of total freedom was ignited in the hearts of all Texans. They no longer wanted a return to the Constitution of 1824. They wanted independence from Mexico.

Davy Crockett was much respected in the Alamo, and if he had left, there is no doubt many others would have followed him. The men knew he was a courageous and tenacious fighter, and without his commitment to stay, the Alamo might have been abandoned without a fight, spelling disaster for General Houston's army. Crockett's brave example led to the freedoms that Texans enjoy today. His commitment to American ideals made him travel to San Antonio and immortality.

Crockett's heroism and courage in accepting death so that others might be free are truly remarkable. I have always tried to follow my convictions, even if I get into occasional trouble. Sometimes, troublesome beliefs and commitments can lead to just and great results. Life does not often draw clear lines in the sand, asking you to step across and accomplish something outstanding. When it does, the things to which you are committed will show the way.

Only those who make their feet follow their hearts deserve respect. Belief leads to commitment and commitment dictates my actions. That is why Davy Crockett is my hero.

CONGRESSMAN TODD TIAHRT

CONGRESS OF THE UNITED STATES

HOUSE OF REPRESENTATIVES

THE FOURTH DISTRICT OF KANSAS

In the 1994 congressional election, Tiahrt defied the political pundits and ran against an eighteen-year congressional incumbent. While running a tight and frugal campaign and spending less than $200,000, Tiahrt upset his opponent.

A native of Vermillion, South Dakota, Tiahrt worked on the family farm with a brother and two sisters. He attended public schools and graduated with a bachelor of arts degree from Evangel College in Missouri. While at Evangel, he met his wife, Vicki. They moved to Wichita, Kansas, in 1981. Tiahrt received his MBA in marketing from Southwest Missouri State. He worked for the Boeing Company for thirteen years until elected to Congress.

His political career began in 1990 when he challenged a Kansas state house incumbent. He lost the election by only eight votes. He tried again in 1992 for a Kansas senate seat and won. Tiahrt was an active state senator, compiling an impressive record as a freshman and serving on several committees.

The Tiahrts live in the Wichita area with their three children,

Jessica, John, and Luke. They are active in the local public school system, their church, and Kansas Republican politics.

Congressman Tiahrt is a member of the National Security and Science Committees and serves on four subcommittees.

How to Contact

1319 Longworth House Office Building, Washington, D.C. 20515
Telephone: 202-225-6216
Fax: 202-225-3489

☆ ☆ ☆ ☆ ☆ ☆ ☆ ☆ ☆ ☆ ☆ ☆ ☆

One of the intellectual vacuums created in our century has been the loss of our ability to transfer wisdom from one generation to the next. Our older citizens feel this acutely, while our younger people often do not know what they are missing until it is too late.

Most of us take for granted family members and friends with whom we spend our time, and we do not realize the value of the moments until we're apart. My grandfather on my mother's side of the family, John William Steele, made a profound impression on my life. Grandpa Steele lived to be ninety-four years old, and he was the embodiment of a person who took great pride and great pleasure in his work. He passed to me and all his grandchildren a legacy of excellence in the workplace. Grandpa wrote the book on exemplary work ethics and a positive attitude on life.

As I look back on the history of my family and our times together, I am struck by Grandpa's level of responsibility to claim his ownership of decisions and actions that affected the well-being of us all. His was not a life without its portion of hardships and sorrows, but Grandpa didn't spend time feeling sorry for himself or musing over what might have been. His love for the land, and for the work itself, inspired his can-do, must-do attitude. I like to think at least some of that character has rubbed off on me.

I have a photocopy of a diary that my grandmother, Jessie Braden Steele, left to my mother. It tells of my grandparents' life in South Dakota and how Grandpa and his brother migrated from Iowa to South Dakota at the turn of the century. Grandpa took only one major journey in his entire life; it was a train ride around the West Coast. He fell in love with the beauty of the mountains, but ultimately, he decided to build his life in the flats, along the Missouri River bottoms, near Meckling, South Dakota.

John Steele and his brother married two sisters, and they all lived together while they constructed their homesteads. Grandmother's diary gives us a picture of what life was like on the plains nearly one hundred years ago, growing up in Sioux territory. The local Sioux, curious to observe the new settlers and their strange ways, had a habit of walking through the Steele household at will. Grandmother wrote that once, while she was standing in the kitchen with her back to the door, a Sioux came silently into the room. When she turned to see what she called "an expressionless warrior" standing before her, she yelped, dropped a mixing bowl, and fled from the house! Grandma was never in any real danger, but she was skeptical all the same. Her diary tells of many a day spent taking refuge in the sanctuary built under the stairwell of their home.

When Grandpa married Jessie Braden, he believed he had "married up" in class. Grandma brought a little dowry to the union, and she was accustomed to the finer things in life. Grandpa worked hard to ensure that his beloved Jessie had nice furniture, crisp linens, delicate china, and silver flatware. Grandpa was happiest when there was a table full of food at Christmastime and a house full of people during the holidays. Although he never entered much into the conversation, he loved to hear the laughter of children and listen to the discussions, and arguments, of the adults.

Sometimes those discussions turned a bit serious, as when Grandpa and his brother got into a fight over the "new road." The Steele brothers had actually built a section of U.S. Highway 50, back when there were only cattle trails connecting many towns. We all learned some new vocabulary words when those two brothers got into it! The other relatives present would just roll their eyes and shrug it off as a family squabble.

It was different when Grandpa mixed it up with the neighbors. A homesteader next door got downright abusive when Grandpa's sheep strayed into his cornfield. I was there that time and ready to do battle in Grandpa's behalf. To my surprise, Grandpa just walked away from the confrontation with little more than a humble, "OK." He later instructed me, "Choose your battles wisely, son. I prefer to knock the chips off my shoulder."

That philosophy has held me in good stead. It is also one of the most important things I have learned from Senator Bob Dole. Today's enemy may be tomorrow's friend. It's never the last floor vote you're worried about; it's the next. That's how you build the coalitions that can make things work.

It is a lesson that Grandpa's uncle, Thomas Jefferson Steele, apparently did not learn. Tom Steele was a congressman from Sioux City, Iowa, in 1914. Two years later, he lost his bid for reelection to a gentleman by the name of George C. Scott. None of his papers survived to the present day, but when I arrived in Washington, D.C., I looked up the records in the archives. I found that Great-great-uncle Steele worked hard to have the first post office established in Sioux City. He also lobbied for an increase in congressional pensions. That last item was probably responsible for his reelection defeat. That revelation resulted in another lesson for me, gleaned from my industrious ancestors; it is an economic lesson of fiscal responsibility and good stewardship.

By midlife, in the 1920s, Grandpa and his business partner–brother had built considerable holdings in farmland, grain elevators, a meat-packing house, and various buildings that housed grocery stores and barbershops; and Grandpa owned half interest in a bank. Then disaster struck. It was universal, bringing despondency and ruin to millions. It was called the Great Depression. Grandpa lost almost everything during those awful years, including his wife, leaving behind two small daughters, the older of which became my mother.

After Grandmother died and the depression took its financial toll on the family, Grandpa poured all his sorrow into hard work. He and his brother retained only two sections of land in the 1930s, but typical of Grandpa's style, he put his nose to the grindstone and worked those two sections back to a productive capacity. To show just how much really hard work that would be, in farming, a section of land is one mile square. Two sections would be two miles wide by one mile long. Now imagine the land has lain untended for years and is not suitable for growing crops. That is the challenge Grandpa faced and had to overcome to survive. At one time, seventeen families worked and found sustenance on that farm, and Grandpa found it very difficult to fire anyone. His method for terminating an employee was piling on the work so the poor farmhand would finally quit.

Grandpa was a solitary man and not one to talk much. He could have been a role model for the strong, silent type characterized by Hollywood. My mother has told me that Grandma made a deathbed plea to Grandpa that he never marry again. She was afraid another woman might not raise their daughters in an appropriate manner. Grandpa honored her request, and it may be the reason why work became his strongest passion.

For Grandpa, all things came to pass, the good times and the bad. He preferred to speak only of the satisfaction and rewards of hard work. Hard work and education, that was the measure of a man! He attended school only until the fourth grade. That was a common experience for children of his era because farms lacked the mechanical helpers we have today, and every extra hand and strong back was needed in the fields and the barn. Grandpa liked to recite the familiar adage, "Get a good, solid education, son. They can never take that away from you."

My fondest memories of Grandpa are of following him around the farm. We would travel from the house to the chicken house to the garden to the feedlot to the barns. I helped when I could, but mostly I just played around him. He was an easy man to be with, and I enjoyed being with him almost as much as he enjoyed assigning me to a routine farm task. I chopped weeds, carried water to the chickens, gathered eggs, took hay to the cattle, and hoed the garden. Often, I would sneak off to play, but our paths would unexpectedly cross and I would fall in line once more. All those endless chores seemed menial to me at the time, but Grandpa's message of perseverance and hard work left its intended mark on me.

Today we hear so much about self-esteem. It is evident from Grandpa's example that one cannot have self-esteem without accomplishment in life. In turn, one cannot have accomplishment without hard work. Success is self-perpetuating. My confidence in one area tells me I can accomplish other goals. Again, it is Grandpa's can-do legacy.

As a young man, I often wondered how a person develops emotional strength. I saw a real contrast in how different people negotiated the price of equipment bought for the farm and the commodities that were sold. In observing Grandpa, I saw the advantage of having a poker face and a calm demeanor. Of course, having no experience in that area, I thought perhaps the best way to develop a poker face was to play poker! One evening I took a deck of cards and placed it before Grandpa on the dining room table. "Grandpa," I said smugly, "teach me how to play poker." True to form, and without showing the slightest emotion, Grandpa reached over, picked up the cards, and slipped them into the pocket of his overalls. Then he quietly shuffled off to his room. That action said so much to me, without a word being spoken.

Sometime later I learned why he would not show me how to play poker. At one point in his life John Steele had spent his leisure time playing cards. He once won a saloon in a card game; but in another session he lost a family farm. Gambling became a problem for him and tainted his reputation so that he was no longer able to secure the business loans needed to carry on his business activities. To work around the situation, his brother and business partner dealt directly with the banks on his behalf.

That proved to be a great shame for Grandpa, but he became a school of knowledge for his children and grandchildren. Adversity can be a good teacher. Witnessing the pain and the loss of those judgments has left a lasting impression on my life. Yet, I know a life without prudent risk can be a lukewarm life. It appears that balance is the better part of valor.

Grandpa died in 1978. He was a man of staunch character, but not without human faults. He was a man of tenacity and perseverance, a man who wouldn't buckle under. He was a man's man. Others who followed him would teach me lessons in honesty, faith, and love of God and country; but the lessons I learned from Grandpa Steele have given me perspective. With focused perspective, I have the advantage of learning from the past while looking toward the future with hope. That's not a bad thing to pass on to the next generation.

CONGRESSMAN
ZACH WAMP

CONGRESS OF THE UNITED STATES
HOUSE OF REPRESENTATIVES

THE THIRD DISTRICT OF TENNESSEE

Prior to his election, Congressman Wamp was a successful commercial and industrial real estate broker. He attended the University of North Carolina at Chapel Hill and the University of Tennessee. Wamp and his wife, Kim, have a son, Weston, and a daughter, Coty.

Wamp's fellow Republican freshmen elected him to represent them on the Majority Steering Committee. House Speaker Newt Gingrich named Wamp to the Minority Issues Task Force and to the Speaker's Task Force on Congressional Reform. Wamp is a member of the executive committee of the National Republican Congressional Committee. He belongs to the following caucuses: TVA, Travel and Tourism, Fair Trade, Pro-Family, Small Business Survival, and National Security. Congressman Wamp is a board member of the conservative-oriented Washington Legal Foundation. He is the original sponsor of the Wamp Congress Act, a bill to reform campaign finance laws and limit the influence of special interest political action committees, which has drawn more House support than any other campaign finance bill.

Congressman Wamp serves on the Science, Transportation and Infrastructure, and Small Business Committees.

How to Contact

> 423 Cannon House Office Building,
> Washington, D.C. 20515
> Telephone: 202-225-3271
> Fax: 202-225-3494

☆ ☆ ☆ ☆ ☆ ☆ ☆ ☆ ☆ ☆ ☆ ☆ ☆

I t has been said that character is what surfaces when someone is under pressure. The Bible talks about pressure when it refers to the tribulations men and women face during a lifetime. The Greek word for tribulation is *thlipsis*, and it carries the idea of a crushing kind of pressure, a serious affliction or distress. We're not talking about the little bumps in the road we face on the highway of life, but the kind of pressure that exists when our very survival is on the line. I am thankful that few of us have known that kind of pressure.

Colonel Roger Ingvalson knows and understands. When you apply pressure to him, what comes out is the unfailing strength of Jesus Christ. I have known no person with greater character than Roger Ingvalson and no better symbol for all that is good about America than this quiet man from Chattanooga, Tennessee. What is this character of Christ? Galatians 5:22 tells us: "But the fruit of the Spirit is love, joy, peace, longsuffering, kindness, goodness, faithfulness, gentleness, self-control."

It wasn't always like that with Ingvalson. He was a thirty-nine-year-old fighter pilot, thoroughly seasoned in his trade and possessing the self-confidence that went with the ability to maneuver a U.S. Air Force F-105 fighter through the skies at more than five hundred miles per hour. Ingvalson commented, "I didn't live an immoral life, but the life of a fighter pilot is a long way from a life of humility." It was the commitment to doing things right, to living on the edge, that God used to reshape Ingvalson's life on a Tuesday morning in May 1968 in the violent sky above North Vietnam.

A convoy of Russian-made trucks was his target on the eighty-seventh mission Ingvalson had flown since January. He inflicted significant damage to the convoy on his first pass in his F-105, but his commitment to perfection would not let him break off and return to base. "There was no way I could leave a target that was not totally destroyed or on fire," Ingvalson recounted, "so I circled back and made one more pass. I was traveling at 550 miles per hour and only fifty feet above the ground when my aircraft was hit by antiaircraft fire. As I tried to climb, I lost control of my plane at seven hundred feet and was forced to eject. I knew that no one had ever ejected at that speed and survived without being all broken up."

Just as the apostle Paul was radically changed by an encounter with Jesus on the Damascus Road, Ingvalson's life-changing experience had arrived: "The next thing I remember was regaining consciousness just in time to put my feet together prior to hitting the ground. Sitting in that rice paddy, I knew God had performed a miracle because I did not have a single broken bone or a single bruise. With the enemy running toward me, I bowed my head and prayed to God that Jesus would take over my life."

It would be nearly five years before Colonel Ingvalson would again enjoy the air of freedom. He was a prisoner of war in North Vietnam. Suffering, anguish, loneliness, and pain became the norm. Two weeks into his captivity, he saw his captors poison an injured pilot who was begging for medical help. One month into his captivity, he was ushered into the terrible confines of the Hanoi Hilton, where he eventually learned that more than 350 Americans were held prisoner. For nearly twenty months he was in solitary confinement.

Ingvalson explained his mental outlook this way: "The Communists were trying to inflict some sort of mental torture on me so I would lose my mind. I think you can imagine what happens to your mind when you are alone in a box for nearly two years. They thought I was alone, but they didn't understand I had a cell mate. Jesus was with me in that cell. Through it all, I had peace and confidence about what was happening to me. He was there the whole time."

The colonel was beaten, chained to his bed, and tortured. On one occasion he was tied up by his jailers in such a way that his elbows were pulled backward until they touched. He painfully recalled, "You could literally feel the cartilage in your chest ripping apart." He related the story of how a ranking officer in another camp was hung by his ankles three feet off the ground and dropped repeatedly on his head as punishment for two Americans who had tried unsuccessfully to escape.

Ingvalson had no Bible, but he had the God of the Bible. Without the help of a single other person, he learned to pray, thank God for his circumstances, and grow spiritually. He was being squeezed, and God was coming out. Dozens of times a day he prayed and recited Psalm 23 and the few other Bible verses he could remember. Nine months after his capture the Vietnamese allowed him to receive mail. In the first letter from his mother, she wrote "Psalm 46:1" at the bottom of a page, but he couldn't remember the passage.

Ingvalson revealed that in the complete absence of the usual Christian study aids, "All I had was faith, and God was being faithful to teach me about Himself. When you are on your death-bed for months and months, you know your survival all goes back to Christ. I learned that He would take care of me, that He would see me through this, and that He had a plan for my life." Shortly after leaving solitary, he was given a Bible for a brief period. He immediately found Psalm 46:1 and read, "God is our refuge and strength, a very present help in trouble."

The lessons he learned from that verse would become extremely important again. Eighteen months later he was told his wife, Jackie, who had been diagnosed with multiple sclerosis shortly after they married in 1959, had died. The pressure reached a climax: "I didn't sleep much; I had a dream that night. Until that point, I had always envisioned Jackie being sick and crippled; however, that night she was healthy and happy. I knew then that God was showing me that Jackie was in heaven with Him."

His five years in a brutal prison were a combination of intense suffering mixed with immense joy at having found real peace in his life. Although he was moved to five of the fourteen camps that made up the central prison system in North Vietnam, he and his resourceful fellow prisoners were able to develop a wide array of secret strategies to communicate with one another. He remembered how sometimes it could take two weeks to complete just one sentence. He talked about the joy of spending time praying and singing during Sunday services.

At the end of each service, they would all face east, salute, and say the pledge of allegiance: "Facing east, we figured, was the fast way to get back home to where that great flag flies." I could tell it was a powerful moment for him as he described Christmas Day 1972 and how a fellow prisoner recited the entire story of the birth of Christ from Luke 2. "I never once worried about dying," Ingvalson proclaimed, "because I knew where I was going."

On March 14, 1973, Colonel Roger Ingvalson stepped back once again onto American soil. Gone was the swagger of the fighter pilot, replaced by a willing servant of the God who had seen him through incredible suffering. Gone was the person who lived close to the edge, and in his place was a quiet man who chose to live close to God. Gone was the man who possessed a great deal of knowledge about Jesus, born again into a man who accepted Jesus as his personal Lord and Savior. Gone was the man who focused on himself, transformed to a man whose heart sought only to serve others. The pressure was off, and God's peace was in control.

What Roger Ingvalson has done with his life in the years since he left the military is evidence of what it means to live a life in the way God has called us. Less than a year after returning home, he married Booncy, the widow of his best friend Wayne Fullam, shot down and killed in Vietnam in October 1967. They spent more than a decade caring for Fullam's mother and father, moving them to an apartment near their home in Chattanooga. Roger and Booncy spent months tending to the needs of Fullam's father on his deathbed.

Ingvalson explained, "People who do not believe in God think it is very strange what Booncy and I did for Wayne's parents, but that is the love of Christ dwelling in us that makes us not only want to do that, but enjoy doing that." Ingvalson has spoken in almost every state in America, literally from sea to shining sea. He shares his love for God and country through the testimony of what God did for him during his years in a communist prison. Every two years, he travels to a reunion with the men who suffered with him. He humbly acknowledges that many men today share the love of God after hearing how he survived during those five years in prison. He is truly burdened for those who have chosen a different path for their lives.

Inspired by the work of Chuck Colson, Ingvalson founded the Chattanooga Prison Ministries in 1979. For more than fourteen years the retired colonel ministered to prisoners, ex-prisoners, and their families throughout Tennessee. One on one, he let God use him to change their lives and help those who were hurting. There is something about knowing what it is like to be locked up in a jail that makes his words believable. He said, "There was a time in my life when I believed that if someone got out of line with the law that we should just lock him up and throw away the key. But now I know that Jesus understood my suffering, and I understand the suffering of people all around me, especially those in prison." During his tenure at CPM, Ingvalson mended lives and shared the good news of Jesus with thousands of people. He still hears regularly from ex-prisoners whose lives he touched on his personal road to Damascus.

The list of honors bestowed on Roger Ingvalson establishes his credentials as an American patriot. Among the many he received are the Silver Star for gallantry in action; the Legion of

Merit; the Distinguished Flying Cross with two Oak Leaf Clusters; the Bronze Star with Oak Leaf Cluster for heroic achievement; the Air Medal with six Oak Leaf Clusters; the Air Force Commendation Medal; the Purple Heart with one Oak Leaf Cluster for wounds in combat; the Combat Readiness Medal; the Good Conduct Medal; and the Vietnamese Service for Valor Medal. The list of civilian honors and service organizations that have recognized his accomplishments in Chattanooga includes virtually every major service award available in that city. He has been active in the Christian Businessmen's Committee, which routinely helps businessmen learn how to apply Christian principles in the operation of their business and personal lives.

Today, Roger Ingvalson enjoys traveling with Booncy, being a doting grandfather, serving God's house by being an elder in Chattanooga's largest Presbyterian church, and going on short mission trips. In the fall of 1995, he embarked on a three-week mission trip to the formerly Communist Ukraine, a part of the defunct U.S.S.R. Instead of harboring animosity toward the people whose previous rulers were in many ways responsible for his suffering, Ingvalson reached out to them to share the love of Christ. With Bibles in hand, he went to help elementary school teachers learn how to teach Christian morals and ethics to their children through the Bible.

Just as God directed his first steps out of that Vietnamese rice paddy in 1968, He is still directing the steps of Roger Ingvalson today. Reluctantly, Ingvalson tells of his sufferings only because God uses his story to help others. He loves his God and his country, "the greatest nation, people, and flag on earth," he proudly says of America.

It is not likely he will again face pressures anything like those he endured during the five years in a North Vietnamese prison; but if he should, what will come out even more powerful than before will be the character of Jesus Christ.

CONGRESSMAN
DAVE WELDON

CONGRESS OF THE UNITED STATES
HOUSE OF REPRESENTATIVES

THE FIFTEENTH DISTRICT OF FLORIDA

Representative Dave Weldon is a Brevard County resident who had a private practice in internal medicine in Melbourne, Florida. Born on Long Island, New York, Weldon worked his way through college and graduated Phi Beta Kappa from the State University of New York at Stony Brook with a bachelor of science degree in biochemistry. He met his wife, Nancy, while they were both students at Stony Brook. Following his graduation from Stony Brook, Weldon began studying medicine at the State University of New York at Buffalo's School of Medicine on a scholarship with the Army Health Professions Scholarship program. Following his medical training, Dr. Weldon served a three-year tour of duty with the U.S. Army at Fort Stewart, Georgia. He remained in the U.S. Army Reserves for five years after leaving active duty. Dr. Weldon went into private practice with the Melbourne Internal Medicine Associates, a thirty-eight-member multispecialty medical group in Florida.

In 1989, Dr. Weldon helped found the Space Coast Family

Forum, a citizens' committee established to promote family-related issues in the public arena. He has been actively involved in medical, civic, and church organizations, continually working to help the less fortunate.

Dr. Weldon, his wife, Nancy, and daughter, Katie, reside in Alexandria, Virginia. Weldon is an avid jogger and enjoys sailing and tennis. He relaxes by playing his acoustical guitar.

In the 104th Congress, Representative Weldon serves on the Science Committee and is vice chairman of the Space and Aeronautics Subcommittee, where he represents his aerospace constituents from Florida's Space Coast, home of NASA's Kennedy Space Center and Cape Canaveral Air Station. Additionally, he serves on the Economic and Educational Opportunities Committee, where he champions educational reform issues. Congressman Weldon is also a leader of the freshman class, serving as the freshman representative on the Republican Policy Committee.

How to Contact

216 Cannon House Office Building,
Washington, D.C. 20515
Telephone: 202-225-3671
Fax: 202-225-3516

☆☆☆☆☆☆☆☆☆☆☆☆☆☆

History has given dubious credit to Sir John Hawkins, reportedly the first Englishman to transport slaves to the New World in the year 1562. Hawkins was at first denounced by Queen Elizabeth who called the selling of human beings "detestable." Later, she became astutely aware that with little investment, huge profits by Englishmen could be made plying the slave routes, and the evil practice grew and spread. Two hundred seventy years would pass before it ended.

The man most responsible for halting the English slave trade was William Wilberforce, first elected to Parliament in 1780. He made the fight to stop slavery a battle that consumed his entire public life. As a young man, he decided it was wrong and petitioned for its repeal throughout his lengthy career in Parliament. Not until he was in his seventies did he see it finally ended. His example of determination and persistence, two hundred years ago, is a beacon of encouragement in my life today.

My interest in politics began during college when I took a series of elective political science and history courses. I contemplated abandoning my biochemistry major and plans for medical school to pursue law and politics. After much careful thought, I decided to stay in the biochemistry program and went on to medical school; after six years in the Army medical corps, I entered private practice in internal medicine in Florida.

In the Army I began to feel that our political system and many of the people running our government were failing us. The spiraling debt had the potential to bankrupt our nation. The breakdown of the American family was playing a key role in the rising tide of drug abuse, declines in educational achievement, and increased juvenile crime. Our leaders were not seriously addressing these problems, and many of their programs were making matters worse. The best example is the welfare system that I believe plays a dominant role in undermining family structure by

subsidizing illegitimacy and encouraging social problems. Strong families make strong communities, states, and nations. So-called innovative programs, emanating from a central government in Washington, do not.

I continue to believe strongly that the legalized practice of abortion is very wrong and runs directly counter to the principles upon which our nation was founded. Thomas Jefferson turned the colonial world upside down when he declared that we are "endowed by [our] Creator with certain unalienable rights" and included not only liberty and the pursuit of happiness, but also *the right to life*. Legalized abortion contradicts that principle. Our nation is not united by geography, race, or ethnic origins. We are united by our principles and beliefs, chief of which is the respect for human life. When as a people we begin to abandon these founding doctrines, we may not survive as a nation.

In the fall of 1989, I felt I needed to do something to try to turn some of these problems around. One morning I was playing tennis with a fellow who was head of the local chapter of the National Right to Life Committee when he informed me that our local state legislative delegation was pro-choice. It seemed to them that being pro-life was a losing platform. I was very surprised to learn this because I knew that Ronald Reagan, George Bush, and our pro-life governor Bob Martinez had all carried the district with large majorities.

A few months later I met an engineer by the name of Dana Gartzke. He shared many of my opinions, and together with a group of friends, we decided to form an active political committee to promote family and pro-life values in the political arena. We called ourselves the Space Coast Family Forum because the coastal area encompassing Kennedy Space Center and the Cape Canaveral Air Station is called Florida's Space Coast. In the summer of 1990 we interviewed several political candidates to

determine their positions, then endorsed thirteen of them in the September primary election.

Our group was small and unknown, but when eleven of the thirteen won, I suddenly found myself on the front page of the local newspaper. As one could expect, there were the usual claims that we were forcing our values on others by being involved and that we could not "legislate morality." (Opponents have never properly explained why we can legislate immorality by approving such things as nude bars and X-rated movie houses, and then be incapable of legislating morality.)

Then it was Election Day, November 1990. Many people believed eleven candidates on the ballot would not have been there if it had not been for my efforts and those of the Family Forum. Much to our disappointment, only two of them won! After they led the pack in the primary, I expected our candidates to do better than that. The heavy criticism I received was less than encouraging. Many people on both sides of the political aisle claimed that our positions were "too out of the mainstream" and that our candidates might be able to win in a primary but could not win in a general election.

During that period of discouragement, Robyn Gleason, a woman who had helped me considerably with Family Forum, lent me a book about a former member of the British Parliament, William Wilberforce. When she first told me about Wilberforce, I was quite skeptical, but the more I read about him, the more engrossed with his character I became.

He is not recognized as a major figure in British politics, nor is he often discussed in civil rights circles. Yet historians credit him as being the man most responsible for ending the slave trade in the British Empire. Knowing that we in America had fought a long and bloody war to achieve the same ends, I was eager to learn more about how the British were able to do it peacefully. Finding that his fight to end slavery had taken the better part of his lifetime piqued my interest.

Wilberforce was a Christian man of small physical stature and humble bearing. He did not enjoy good health. His biographers describe a chronic intestinal condition that plagued him his entire life. He decided at an early age that slavery was wrong, a decision no doubt grounded in his Christian beliefs and values. Meeting a young slave boy his own age, who was forced to wear a silver collar around his neck, moved Wilberforce deeply, and he purposed in his heart to fight slavery.

Slave trading in England was a brutal business. Slave ship captains would depart England loaded down with rum, iron, and cloth to trade for slaves with the tribal chiefs in West Africa. Many Africans were cast into slavery by other Africans, who kidnapped them and sold them to the slavers. Of course, they would never have been kidnapped were it not for the traders being there to instigate the cruel practice. The traders would then carry their ill-gained cargo to the Americas and the West Indies, where the slaves were forever sentenced to a life of toil on the plantations.

On the brutal "middle passage," across the southern Atlantic Ocean, one-third to one-half of the slaves died from the inhumane conditions on the ships. They were shackled, ankle to ankle, and packed into the holds, often with so little living space they spent the entire voyage lying on their sides.

The slave traders were nearly as barbaric with their own men. The cheapest commodity on board was human life, as evidenced by the deaths of up to one-third of the crews on many voyages. In contrast, the death rate for non–slave trade merchant sailors was only 2 percent. No doubt the slavers were motivated by the fact they did not pay the crew until they returned to England. A dead sailor did not have to be paid, and there were no survivors' benefits for their families.

Wilberforce was working against the most powerful financial

and political forces in England when he decided to make ending slavery his career goal. Some of the wealthiest men in the British Empire benefited from slavery; they also had full control of the House of Commons and House of Lords. Fortunately, Wilberforce had steadfast allies on his side, notably Prime Minister William Pitt and, later, Prime Minister Charles James Fox. Pitt and Wilberforce were bitter political enemies, but they shared a common hatred of slavery. Pitt met with him in 1787 and recommended that he "give notice to the House of Commons that [he intended] to bring forward the subject of slavery."

Soon after, King George III decreed that a committee of the Privy Council should investigate the slave trade. Predictably, the investigation did not go well. Members of the House of Lords, along with the slave traders, presented evidence that the business was not nearly as bad as opponents claimed. They went as far as to portray the brutal and deadly middle passage as a "joyous and happy occasion" for their hapless passengers.

In 1789, Wilberforce introduced legislation to ban the trade. Hearings were held, but just as it appeared that the momentum was in their favor, a violent revolution rocked France. As fighting broke out in Paris, a slave uprising also occurred in the French West Indian colony of Santo Domingo. Two thousand white people were killed and a thousand plantations destroyed. The news was devastating to the abolitionist cause, and the bill lost on a vote of 163 to 88. How sadly ironic that at the very moment slavery opponents were nearing victory, rebelling slaves doomed history's first attempt to free them.

Discouraged but not defeated, Wilberforce again introduced antislavery legislation in 1792. As before, the bill was hotly debated, and many attempts were made to weaken it by adding toothless amendments. Despite a valiant effort, the final House of Commons bill called for a gradual end to the trade by 1796. As in the United States, where a bill must pass both the House and the

Senate, Wilberforce's bill had to run the same gauntlet in the House of Lords. It was not until 1807, twenty-seven years after he entered Parliament, that the slave trade was permanently abolished. Shortly after its passage, though pleased by the results of the historic legislation, Wilberforce made no attempt to hide the fact that his real goal was not just the abolition of the slave trade, but the ending of slavery itself.

He faced a very difficult reelection in 1807. Wilberforce was an independent, and though he had become a national hero, he faced two well-financed opponents, one a Tory and the other a Whig. The election was close, but Wilberforce won narrowly, enabling him to resume his work in the House of Commons.

The need to bring an immediate end to slavery after the trading in slaves was outlawed became apparent to supporters of the abolitionist movement. Slave traders continued to traffic in slaves despite the law banning it. Many of the men were exceedingly heartless. Most notable was the inhumane Captain Homans. His ship, the *Brillante*, had a crew of sixty. With ten mounted guns, he successfully fought off warships of the British navy. Finally, Homans and his ship, with six hundred slaves on board, was trapped by four heavily armed British warships. As the royal vessels waited for daybreak so the sailors could board his ship, Homans had all six hundred slaves brought to the deck and shackled to the ship's anchor chain.

At dawn, unable to elude the British warships, Homans released the anchor chain. The British sailors could hear the screams of the slaves as they were dragged overboard to their deaths. When Homans's ship was boarded there were no slaves to be found, and he was set free. This story, and many others equally wicked, convinced many in England that slavery must end. Fortunately for Wilberforce, public sentiment moved in his favor, and he was joined in Parliament by other members who shared his opposition. One of the most vocal was Thomas Buxton. In May

1823, Buxton placed the motion on the floor of the House of Commons to end slavery. Wilberforce proudly made the seconding speech.

Wilberforce was called to retire from Parliament in 1825 due to advancing age and the worsening of his chronic health problems. Younger members saw the slavery battle to its conclusion in July 1833. After eight years of debate, the law was carried, officially ending slavery in the British Empire. Only one month later, Wilberforce breathed his last and was laid to rest next to his contemporaries, Prime Ministers Pitt and Fox. Pallbearers at his funeral included the Speaker of the House, the Lord Chancellor of England, and the Duke of Gloucester. Nearly one-third of the nation mourned his passing.

Wilberforce had an inborn compassion that told him slavery was wrong. He possessed the personal force of will to persevere through a lifetime of adversity and witness the death of slavery shortly before his own. The economic loss to the traders and plantation owners was nothing compared to the loss of dignity and freedom they perpetrated against their victims.

After reading about the life of William Wilberforce, I knew there was much to be gained by standing on one's principles and persevering, even when the opposition seems to have the upper hand. The Family Forum I helped found had a few more successes in the 1992 election cycle. We gradually expanded our membership to about 1,500 people who were receiving our mailings regularly.

In the spring of 1994, I felt I could no longer work quietly in the background to affect our nation. Though the Family Forum held a successful candidate forum in April, where several gubernatorial and congressional hopefuls were heard, I began to believe that my role was in the race and not on the sidelines. In May, I entered the contest for Congress. After a hard-fought seven-way primary in September and a runoff election in October, I was able to prevail in the general election. It is truly an honor and privilege to serve in the United States Congress as the representative from Florida's Fifteenth District, the home of America's historic Kennedy Space Center.

As I sit in that grand chamber in the House, I can look back and say there was a time in the fall of 1990 when I seriously considered ending my involvement in politics and devoting myself to my medical practice, my family, and my church. The courageous examples from the life of a man who lived long ago persuaded me otherwise. Reaching forward through time, he awakened in me a new conviction and motivated me never to give up. The values and principles that guided William Wilberforce are desperately needed today.

CONGRESSMAN
ROGER F. WICKER

CONGRESS OF THE UNITED STATES
HOUSE OF REPRESENTATIVES

THE FIRST DISTRICT OF MISSISSIPPI

Congressman Wicker was elected by capturing an impressive 63 percent of the First District vote after a very competitive six-person primary. Wicker is the first Republican to hold the seat since Reconstruction. He was then elected by his congressional colleagues to serve as president of the historic seventy-three-member Republican freshman class of the 104th Congress.

Wicker is the son of former circuit judge Fred and Mrs. Wicker and is a native of Pontotoc, Mississippi. He was educated in the public schools and received his bachelor of arts and law degrees from the University of Mississippi. He served on active duty in the U.S. Air Force and is a lieutenant colonel in the Air Force Reserve. In 1987, Wicker became the first Republican in this century elected to the state senate from northern Mississippi. He chaired two committees while in the state senate. He also served as counsel to Representative Trent Lott on the House Rules Committee in 1980–82.

Wicker is active in his community and is a member of the

Community Development Foundation and the Lions Club. He teaches Sunday school at the First Baptist Church and is a former chairman of the deacons. Wicker lives in Tupelo with his wife, Gayle, and their three children, Margaret, Caroline, and McDaniel.

Representative Wicker's northern First District has been home to such diverse personalities as writers William Faulkner and John Grisham and entertainers Elvis Presley and Morgan Freeman. Important area industries include furniture manufacturing and other forest-related products. It is also home to Ole Miss, the University of Mississippi.

Congressman Wicker is a member of the House Appropriations Committee and three subcommittees.

How to Contact
> 206 Cannon House Office Building,
> Washington, D.C. 20515
> Telephone: 202-225-4306
> Fax: 202-225-3549

☆ ☆ ☆ ☆ ☆ ☆ ☆ ☆ ☆ ☆ ☆ ☆ ☆

If the ordinary man and woman of the republic have character, the future of the republic is assured; and if in its citizenship rugged strength and fealty to the common welfare are lacking, then no brilliancy of intellect and no piled-up material prosperity will avail to save the nation from destruction.

—Theodore Roosevelt

The life of Theodore Roosevelt—president, adventurer, naturalist, author—has been an inspiration to generations of Americans. His rugged independence, pioneering spirit, forth right style, and commanding presence are the same traits that, in large measure, have defined American culture and the way we view ourselves as a nation.

Although many distinguishing qualities may be used in describing Roosevelt, none is more appropriate than perseverance, a trait that he developed through events in his childhood. As a young boy growing up in New York City, Roosevelt's life was marked with the troubling effects of asthma as well as extreme nearsightedness. Some of the future president's earliest memories must have included the all too often sleepless nights filled with violent coughing spasms, hyperventilating, and a feeling of strangulation followed by a midnight carriage ride to enable the lad's lungs to return to normal. Very little accurate information was available concerning the disease of bronchial asthma when young Roosevelt—known by his family and close friends as Teedie—first displayed symptoms at the age of four. In overcoming his malady through the years, Teedie demonstrated much of the dogged determination that would eventually take him to the heights of power.

In a different or lesser person his physical problems might have been accommodated. After all, Teedie showed an interest in science and nature, which might have resulted in a life of relatively easy travel and the indoor work of a laboratory scientist. But such a destiny was not a part of the young man's makeup. He would fight to overcome the weakness in his lungs; he would never allow his defective eyesight to become an actual disability.

Young Theodore Roosevelt gradually, but steadily, came around to the conclusion of his father concerning the importance of rigorous physical development. "You have the mind but not the body," said the senior Roosevelt, "and without the help of the body, the mind cannot go as far as it should. You must *make* your body." Encouraged by his father, the twelve-year-old lad began a dreary and lengthy regimen of fitness training with dumbbells, horizontal bars, and a punching bag in a gym constructed at the family residence.

Two years later he took up boxing lessons after a humiliating incident in which four other boys taunted him and demonstrated young Roosevelt's complete physical inferiority as he attempted to fight back. His enthusiasm for boxing continued until the end of his first term as president when he was hit in the left eye during a sparring session with a young army officer. It was only after a stern admonishment from a Washington ophthalmologist that he gave up the sport in order to save whatever vision remained in his injured eye. Four years later, when he finally lost the use of his left eye, he kept it a closely guarded secret.

As Roosevelt arrived at his midteens, he eventually began to excel in sports, claiming victories in such track-and-field events as racing, broad jumping, and pole vaulting. A great portion of his physical strengthening and maturation occurred at his family's residence at Oyster Bay on Long Island, where the young man learned to ride horses and become a crack shot.

In his view, the personal lessons he learned early in his life had greater influence on Roosevelt than his highly touted Harvard education. Later in life, he referred to a favorite magazine, *Our Young Folks*, "which taught me much more than any of my textbooks." One criticism of his own experience with higher education was "that it failed to instill into youth the individual virtues . . . the necessity of character."

His inner need to persevere and overcome weak health is an integral part of the character of the man whom millions of people around the world would later come to know and admire. In his Pulitzer Prize–winning biography, Henry F. Pringle captured this indefatigable quality. "The boy detested his puny body," stated Pringle. "In those days of childhood illness lies the clue to the evangelical vitality of later years. Theodore Roosevelt, by unending persistence, developed his body to outward strength. Anyone who did less was a weakling. Anyone who did less was no true patriot." Pringle found in Roosevelt's drive for rugged strength "the Gospel of Strenuousity," evidenced by "extraordinary rambles through streams and gorges in which the President of the United States led a file of panting, sweating, silently cursing diplomats, army officers, and Cabinet members."

Without the spirit of perseverance, without the transcending of physical incapacity, Teddy Roosevelt, the Rough Rider, never would have led a charge up San Juan Hill ("the great day of my life," he called it years later). As it was, in 1898, when America went to war with Spain, the robust thirty-nine-year-old Roosevelt eagerly resigned his position as assistant secretary of the navy and volunteered to help organize a group that would become known as the Rough Riders. With only his scant military experience in the New York National Guard to draw upon, Roosevelt personally trained and led the Rough Riders into the heat of battle. The success of Theodore Roosevelt in the Spanish-American War led directly to his winning the governorship of New York later that year and to the vice presidency under William McKinley two years later.

As a footnote to his character, it is important to acknowledge that while he enjoyed the personal benefits of his military accomplishments for the balance of his career, he remained at all times fully committed to the men of the Rough Riders. Upon their triumphant return to New York, Roosevelt warned the veterans, "Don't get gay and pose as heroes. Don't go back and lie on your laurels; they'll wither." Later, he attended Rough Rider reunions, found jobs for unemployed veterans, and occasionally even kept them out of jail. Roosevelt developed such a deep affection for his men and his military position that even after leaving the presidency, he asked to be referred to as Colonel Roosevelt.

Roosevelt's perseverance in his personal life carried over into his political life, where he was able to draw from the determination he had developed while struggling against asthma and fighting the Spaniards.

Roosevelt demonstrated his straightforward personality during his tenure as Civil Service commissioner. Previous commissioners had been doomed to the ridicule of Congress, but Roosevelt took the position as a personal challenge. He stood up for competent working men and women and focused his substantial aggressiveness on corruption and mismanagement in the federal bureaucracy. When he began the task in 1889, the Civil Service was an easy target for senators and congressmen who needed to shore up their constituencies. By the end of his service as commissioner in 1895, word had spread of his tough but fair policies, and the majority of public support had swung to Roosevelt. The American people began to admire his tenacity and fearlessness, while the Washington establishment at least learned to acknowledge and respect those traits. Where Washington's fast-paced life would have led other men to compromise their integrity, Roosevelt's character was strengthened and enriched by his experiences.

Theodore Roosevelt's strength of character eventually carried him to the presidency, but he remained grounded in common values. For example, as president, he proposed a "Square Deal" for every American in an effort to protect the average American worker from exploitation. Roosevelt said, "When I say I believe in a square deal I do not mean, and probably nobody that speaks the truth can mean, that he believes it possible to give every man the best hand. If the cards do not come to any man, or if they do come, and he has not got the power to play them, then that is his affair. All I mean is that there shall be no crookedness in the dealing." Roosevelt maintained a commitment to rank-and-file citizens, and he had the dogged perseverance to effect worthwhile change on their behalf.

While often quoted, Roosevelt is most widely remembered for his fondness of the West African proverb, "Speak softly and carry a big stick; you will go far." As Pringle pointed out, this expression—first in describing his attitude toward the New York Republican political machine and later as his slogan in dealing with foreign governments—pervaded Roosevelt's political life. This motto comes to mind when many people think about Roosevelt, yet an incident during a hunting trip to Mississippi displays another side of him. Roosevelt led an expedition near the city of Vicksburg in search of the elusive black bear. After some time with no success, a motherless bear cub wandered through the hunting party's sights. When the president could not bring himself to shoot the abandoned cub, the popular nickname "Teddy Bear" was born.

Because of the debilitating nature of his illness early in life, Roosevelt pursued activities during times of comparative health with even more zest than otherwise would have been the case. Faced with uncertain health in the future, young Roosevelt wanted to squeeze as much activity and exercise as possible into those days when he was feeling well. Later in life, Roosevelt risked more than $50,000 of his inheritance to buy land in the South Dakota Territory. He lost most of his investment, but he profited tenfold from the clean, open air and the personal friendships established with cattlemen and ranchers. In the Wild West, it became evident that he had the ability to lead men of every walk with genuine sincerity and an uncompromising personality.

Even in his later years, Roosevelt continued to look for challenges. In early 1917, at the age of fifty-eight, he petitioned President Wilson for the right to lead a division on the European western front in the First World War, a request that was denied in spite of bipartisan recommendations on Roosevelt's behalf. Their former rivalry must have made such a request rather delicate for Wilson, but his decision was easily justified. The War College Division frowned on the recommissioning of someone who had not received up-to-date command training.

French Premier G. B. E. Clemenceau, in a final appeal to Wilson, pointed out the enormous morale boost that would undoubtedly result from Theodore Roosevelt's assignment to the front. Clemenceau flatly told Wilson that Colonel Roosevelt's name was "one which sums up the beauty of American intervention. He is an idealist, imbued with simple, vital idealism." He went on to remind the president, "You are too much of a philosopher to ignore that the influence on the people of great leaders of men often exceeds their personal merits, thanks to the legendary halo surrounding them. The name of Roosevelt has this legendary force in our country."

To the end of his life, Roosevelt continued to have a profound impact on the character of our nation. Theodore Roosevelt embodied the virtues that have come to be associated with the American spirit—shining integrity, gallant adventurism, and uncompromising honesty. Yet what distinguishes Theodore Roosevelt as a most remarkable American hero is the perseverance of his courage and character beyond a single moment and across a lifetime.